Excerpts from unsolicited letters and e-mails received by Freedom In Christ Ministries from people who have received the teaching in this series:

I can truly say tha  *r, entering into the fullness of my* *n the most significant moment o*

The release that I feu as years of shame and bondage were lifted from me is hard to describe. I really do not know what to say – I feel like a human being again!

My life has been transformed. It truly was like walking from darkness back into light again.

FICM provided the tool which has allowed me to break the sin-repent-cycle. I am full of hope for the future.

I am a new person and everyone has seen the difference.

Even though I work for a church and have done many things for God, my walk had become a laboured trudge. Yet now I feel so at peace.

I have a clear head, praise Jesus – it hadn't been clear for years!

Finding my freedom in Christ has changed my life.

The everyday problems of life that once seemed so insurmountable are now well in perspective and I am able to tackle most of them in a calm and rational way.

It has transformed my life. I now know God always loves me even though sometimes I might stray from the path he has mapped out for me. I know God is always there, and I marvel at the truth about his kindness, his generosity, and his feelings towards me.

When my ex-husband left, I felt like half a person. I didn't think I should be alone and I didn't feel whole. Those feelings have gone. I feel fulfilled in who I am and am happy with my life.

FREEDOM IN CHRIST

Discipleship Series   **BOOK 4**

THE YOU GOD PLANNED

DON'T LET ANYTHING OR ANYONE HOLD YOU BACK

STEVE GOSS

MONARCH
BOOKS
Oxford, UK & Grand Rapids, Michigan, USA

First published in the UK 2008 by Monarch Books
(a publishing imprint of Lion Hudson plc),
Wilkinson House, Jordan Hill Road, Oxford OX2 8DR.
Tel: +44 (0)1865 302750   Fax: +44 (0)1865 302757
monarch@lionhudson.com
www.lionhudson.com

Reprinted 2011.

ISBN: 978-1-85424-860-2 (UK)
ISBN: 978-0-8254-6192-7 (USA)

Distributed by:
UK: Marston Book Services Ltd, PO Box 269, Abingdon, Oxon OX14 4ᵛ
USA: Kregel Publications, PO Box 2607,Grand Rapids, Michigan 495ᶠ

British Library Cataloguing Data
A catalogue record for this book is available from the British Library.

Printed and bound in Great Britain by Clays Ltd, St Ives plc.

This book is dedicated to Emilia,
a gentle and caring young lady who is absolutely committed
to truth and integrity. I so appreciate her willingness
to speak out boldly and plainly.

Contents

A Special Word of Thanks

I have learned just about everything I know about helping people become fruitful disciples from Neil Anderson, author of *The Bondage Breaker*, *Victory Over the Darkness* and many other books. These are now regarded by many Christians as classics, and rightly so.

It has been my immense privilege to spend time with Neil, to sit under his teaching at many conferences, to collaborate with him in writing *The Freedom In Christ Discipleship Course*, and to have the opportunity to put my questions to him while we were 'on the road' together.

One of the first things I did when I sensed that the Lord might be prompting me to write this series, was to ask Neil if he minded. After all, the way he has taught these great biblical principles of freedom is so much part of me now, that I could not possibly write these books without using his fundamental methodology.

He had every right to say no and if he had done that I would have dropped the project there and then. However, he positively encouraged me to get started.

For that, and for all he has taught to so many over the years, I am indebted to this man of God who continues to travel the world with this life-changing message.

My thanks go too to Tony Collins and Rod Shepherd at Monarch for their help in getting this series off the ground, as well as to the fantastic team at Freedom In Christ Ministries for their constant support and sacrificial service in taking this message to churches around the country.

Foreword

For twenty-five years I believed in God and regularly attended church. If anyone asked me about my beliefs, I told them that I was a Christian. I looked like a Christian and generally acted like one. In Europe and North America if one respected their parents and wanted to be a 'good boy or girl' it was the cultural thing to be and do. It is sobering to look back and realize that I was one of those millions of cultural 'Christians' who don't have an authentic relationship with their Creator and Heavenly Father. If God hadn't intervened in my life I would have become like the rest of those disillusioned by religion and joined the pagan parade now exiting the culturally or politically correct "church."

Religion is the curse of this world, and the force behind many of the conflicts plaguing the planet. However, a relationship with God is our only hope. I was the senior warden of an Episcopal (Anglican) Church and working as an aerospace engineer when I was invited to attend a lay institute for evangelism. I didn't know what that was and had I known I probably wouldn't have gone. The priest wanted me to go with him. So I did, and while learning to share my faith I realized I didn't have any. The presenter asked what difference it would make in our religious beliefs if Christ hadn't come in the flesh? I didn't have an answer. I believed in God and that was enough. Wasn't it?

I heard the gospel for the first time, and gladly gave my heart to Christ and was born again. I became a new creation in Christ, but it took me several years to fully understand what that really meant. At first I was really excited about my new-found faith, and at the same time disappointed in myself for playing 'church' all those years. I couldn't help but wonder how many others were going through the same motions and missing the real relationship that God wants us to have with himself.

11

Two years later I sensed the call of God to go into full time ministry. The past forty years have been an exciting adventure of learning, growing, and discovering how God sets captives free and binds up their broken hearts. My dear friends and colleagues, Steve and Zoë Goss, have been going through the same transformation and now God is using them to accomplish his work in the United Kingdom.

In writing these four discipleship books, Steve has done a masterful work in presenting the core message of Freedom In Christ Ministries. You will learn, as we have, what difference Christ makes in our 'religious beliefs'. Jesus is the One who died for the sin that has separated us from God. Jesus rose from the dead in order that we can have new life in him. His sacrificial life, death and resurrection also disarmed the god of this world (Colossians 2:15). Jesus came to undo the works of Satan (1 John 3:8) who has deceived the world (Revelation 12:9), and has it under his control (1 John 5:19).

The Church is not an institution for religious observances. It is not an organization, it is an organism. The Church is the body of Christ. The membership is made up of born-again believers who are alive and free in Christ. Their names are written in the Lamb's book of life. 'As many as received him, to them he gave the right to become children of God, to those who believe in his name' (John 1:12). You will discover this and much more as you work your way through this series of discipleship books. So welcome to the family of God. You have many spiritual brothers and sisters in Christ who are learning and growing just as you are. "The Holy Spirit is bearing witness with your spirit that you are a child of God" (Romans 8:16). Have you ever considered what an incredible privilege it is to be called a child of God? The grace of God is truly amazing, and may you grow in that grace and become all that your Heavenly Father created you to be.

Dr. Neil T. Anderson
Founder and President Emeritus of Freedom In Christ Ministries

It's the First Day of the Rest of Your Life

As I write this, I am coming to the end of a week's holiday in a house whose garden backs onto the ninth hole of the famous golf course in Le Touquet in northern France. It's a bit wasted on me because I've never played golf in my life. However, I woke up unusually early this morning, and went for a walk on the course before the golfers were let loose on it.

Having marvelled at the sunrise, I took the opportunity to walk the length of the ninth hole and work out what you would have to do if you were to play it. It's a par four, which means that a reasonably good player should take four shots to complete it. Having tried my hand at crazy golf yesterday, and noted that you have to go over a ditch and round a corner to reach the green, I can't help feeling that I would take a lot more shots than that and do some damage to the carefully manicured turf!

As I went to have a look at the hole itself, it struck me that, once you have potted your ball at the ninth hole, you are exactly half way around the course. I must be feeling my age because I found myself thinking, 'I'm probably at least half way through my life. It's as if I have nine holes behind me and nine still to go. What's on my scorecard for the first nine holes? How have I done so far?'

Interesting question! How would you judge your 'scorecard' so far? More importantly, how would God judge it? And would he use the same criteria?

The wonderful thing about our God, of course, is that, no matter how badly you have messed up so far, whatever the

13

state of your scorecard, you still have the opportunity to finish the remaining holes with a perfect score. If you are a Christian, your past need not determine your future.

In this book we will see that, from here on in, nothing and nobody can stop you becoming the person God wants you to be. Everything is still to play for.

First, however, some bad news.

You are going to die

I heard about a man who had been diagnosed with incurable pancreatic cancer and given less than a year to live. He still felt in good health so he weighed up his options and decided to make the most of the time he had left. He cashed in all his assets, including his pension, and lived a life of luxury. The twelve months passed. Not only was he still alive but he appeared to be in good health. More tests were run and the doctors concluded that his symptoms were not caused by cancer after all but by a different condition that was not life-threatening.

When he heard this, he was initially ecstatic – he had been let off a death sentence. However, once the euphoria had worn off, he had to face reality. He had just blown his life savings. He faced a future with no financial provision. The last I heard, he was looking into the possibility of bringing a legal case against the hospital that treated him.

When my father-in-law was in his early seventies, he was diagnosed with cancer that could be treated but not cured. Although he didn't say so at the time, I'm pretty sure he knew that meant that his remaining time would be limited.

For a couple of years he and my mother-in-law behaved like a honeymoon couple – they had a great time enjoying each other's company and making the most of the time they had left together. I am not sure that would have happened in quite the same way if they had not been given the news that the time they had left together would definitely be cut short.

When you realize that you are definitely going to die, it focuses your mind. You start putting your house in order. Some things that seemed important no longer seem to matter so much. Things that didn't seem important suddenly take on a new significance.

I have some news for you. You are going to die! And that's definite. Well, to be more precise, some of us may simply be caught up to heaven with Jesus when he returns rather than physically die (1 Thessalonians 4:17). Either way, everything is going to change. Your physical life here will be over. It's just as certain as if you had been given a terminal diagnosis by a doctor.

Choose how you will build

Paul gives us a fascinating glimpse of what will happen to Christians on that day, one that is so important that he simply calls it 'the Day'. He tells us that each of us had a foundation laid in our lives when we became Christians, and that foundation is Jesus Christ himself. He then goes on to say:

> If any man builds on this foundation using gold, silver, costly stones, wood, hay or straw, his work will be shown for what it is, because the Day will bring it to light. It will be revealed with fire, and the fire will test the quality of each man's work. If what he has built survives, he will receive his reward. If it is burned up, he will suffer loss; he himself will be saved, but only as one escaping through the flames.
>
> (1 CORINTHIANS 3:12–14)

Each of us has a choice: we can build our lives with good things that will not be burned up (which he likens to gold, silver and precious stones) or with things that will not withstand the test of time (like wood, hay and straw). This passage is clearly not about our salvation. Both those who build with good things and those who build with bad will be saved. But those who build with things that do not last 'will suffer loss', even though they will still be saved. They will be there in glory but only 'as one escaping through the flames'. I imagine them standing there with just a few scraps of burnt clothing, perhaps with their eyebrows singed, looking rather dirty, yet still caught up with the absolute wonder of being in heaven and seeing their heavenly Father face to face.

So, those who build with good things will have some extra reward in heaven over and above their salvation. Compare that to the parable Jesus told where a master gave his servants some money. When he returned, he said to a servant who had put the money to work and made more money, 'Well done, good and faithful servant! You have been faithful with a few things; I will put you in charge of many things' (Matthew 25:21). Those of us who spend our time on earth doing significant things can expect to be given even more significant things in the future. We do not know exactly what that means but one thing is for sure: heaven will not be about sitting around on clouds playing harps. We will be involved in significant things. Paul gives us some idea when he says, 'Do you not know that we will judge angels?' (1 Corinthians 6:3).

I have no desire to be morbid, but it does us no harm whatsoever to ponder the fact that this life is only a temporary phase. It will soon be over. For the Christian, that need not be a scary thought – when we die, it just gets better – but it's a thought that should serve to focus our minds on the rest of our life and what we are going to build with. Are we going to build with things that will stand the test or things that will ultimately be burned up?

If you want to become the person God planned, you will, of course, want to build with good things. But how do you know whether you are building with good things or bad things? Well, some bad things are obvious. The problem we have is with things that we might think are good but which, when all is said and done, turn out to be useless.

Generally speaking, how we behave and what we do in life reflect the goals we are trying to achieve. If your goal is to be rich, most of the things you do will be geared towards making money. If your goal is to be liked, you will invest a lot of time in doing whatever you believe will make others like you.

To become the person God intends you to be, a crucial question to answer is, what is God's goal for the rest of your life? It stands to reason that if we want to build with things that God considers valuable, we need to make sure our goals tie in with his goal for us. If we can find the answer to that and work towards it, we can be sure that we are building with gold, silver and precious stones.

God's Goal for the Rest of Your Life

As I mentioned earlier, I have been writing some of this book while on holiday in France. Last week we were staying right next to a huge church in the centre of a small village in Normandy. On walking through the graveyard, I was struck by two graves next to each other. Both had raised gravestones bearing the details of the people who had been buried there. But on the foot of each gravestone, in very large letters that drew the eye, was the French word '*Regrets*'. I am not sure that this word is the direct equivalent of the English word 'regrets' – I suspect that the regrets referred to were those of the people left behind who were missing their relative. However, it got me wondering. I want the rest of my life to be successful in God's eyes. I don't want to come to the end of my life and look back and feel I have to stamp 'Regrets' on it. Of course, there are bound to be some things I will regret. Some of those things will be beyond my ability to control. But the truth is that from this point on, there is no reason that I should add to them.

If you want the rest of your Christian life to count for eternity, the secret is simple: find out what God's goal for your life is and make sure that your goal is the same.

Of course, we all have more than one goal in our life – at any one time we may be working towards several objectives. But God has one overriding goal for us that he wants to see achieved. If we adopt this one overriding goal and make sure our other goals fall into line with it, we'll be in good shape when 'the Day' comes.

So what is God's goal for the rest of my life?

Characteristics

As we work our way towards an answer, let's apply some logic. What characteristics would a goal from a loving, caring God have? I have listed five below. When we arrive at a conclusion about what God's goal for your life is, we will come back and check that it does indeed have these characteristics:

Measurable
There's no point having a goal if you can't measure how far towards it you have progressed. Indeed, it's clear from 1 Corinthians 3:12–14 that God himself will, in effect, measure up our progress when we stand before him on 'the Day'.

Achievable
If God wants something done, can it be done? In other words, if God has a goal for your life, can it be blocked, or is its fulfilment uncertain or impossible?

To put it another way, would God ever say, in effect, 'I have something for you to do. I know you won't be able to do it, but give it your best shot.' That's ridiculous! It's like saying to your child, 'I want you to mow the lawn. Unfortunately, the lawn is covered with rubble, the mower doesn't work and there's no fuel. But try your best anyway.' Sometimes earthly authority figures do issue commands like that, but when they do, it has the effect of undermining their authority. God does not work like that.

The conclusion we can draw is that, by definition, no God-given goal for your life can ever be impossible, uncertain, or blocked – God would not do that to you. In other words, you can become the person God intends.

Not dependent on other people
Taking that thought further, we can deduce that no God-given goal can be dependent on other people. If it were, they may

choose not to cooperate, and then it would not be a goal that we could definitely achieve. God is absolutely fair and would not ask us to do something that was not completely within our ability to do.

Not dependent on circumstances

Similarly, if the goal God gave us were dependent on circumstances going our way, it would not be fair. We cannot control or influence the circumstances of our life that much. If our goal were dependent on circumstances that we had no right or ability to control, we could never be certain that it would be fulfilled.

Not dependent on how gifted we are

Paul tells us that we are all given different gifts (Romans 12:6–8), and the parable of the talents that Jesus tells in Matthew 25:14–30 implies that we are given different amounts of gifts. Some of us are given ten talents, others just one. If our different gifts or different number of gifts gave one of us an advantage over someone else in reaching our God-given goals, that would not be fair. And one thing we can absolutely depend on is that God is fair. So any goal that he has for us must be equally achievable whether you are a ten-talented or a one-talented person.

So what is the goal?

Let's start to move towards identifying a goal which meets those characteristics. 2 Peter 1:3–10 is a great place to start:

His divine power has given us everything we need for life and godliness through our knowledge of him who called us by his own glory and goodness. Through these he has given us his very great and precious promises, so that through them you may participate in the divine nature and escape the corruption in the world caused by evil desires.

We haven't quite got to the goal yet, but let's stop reading there for a moment, because Peter wants us to understand something very important before he goes on to show us God's goal for our lives. He wants us to understand that any future goal is based on what has already happened – what happened, in fact, at the moment we first turned to Christ and became a Christian. This is the 'foundation' that Paul talked about in 1 Corinthians 3:12–14, which we looked at earlier.

The foundation that has been laid

Peter starts by writing in the past tense. He tells us about things that have already happened.

We have everything we need for life and godliness

This is a mind-blowing statement and we don't have time to do it justice here. If you have read the first three books in this series, however, you will have seen that it is absolutely true.

We face three powerful enemies in the form of the world, the flesh and the devil, but in Christ we are more than a match for all of them. You will also have seen the key role that repentance plays in kicking the enemy's influence out of our life, and how any Christian can do that.

Nowhere in the Bible will you find any suggestion that a Christian needs to ask God for more power to live the Christian life. Why is this? God has already given us everything we need. It does not always feel like that but it is nevertheless true.

What we need for life and godliness was given to us 'through our knowledge of him'. This is reminiscent of Jesus' great statement: 'You will know the truth and the truth will set you free' (John 8:32). At the most basic level, Jesus himself is the Truth. Our knowledge of him, which becomes deeper as we move on in our relationship with him, is where it all starts.

We already participate in God's divine nature

Peter goes on to say that God has given us some great promises. The word is perhaps better translated here as 'assurances'. 'Promises' implies there is more to come, but Peter is at pains here to show us what we already possess.

What does it mean to 'participate in God's divine nature'? This is another thing that blows my mind when I understand its full force. There was a time when who we were – our very nature – was displeasing to God. We were 'objects of wrath' (Ephesians 2:3) – no matter what we did, we could not please God. That has been completely turned around. Through Jesus Christ we have been made holy through and through. In the very depths of our being we are now holy and righteous. In fact, throughout the New Testament Christians are called 'saints', which means 'holy ones'. We are not the same people we once were. We have been completely transformed from the inside out. It is not that we have been covered by the righteousness of Christ but are still the same no-good, rotten people underneath – no, deep down inside we are now lovely and clean, made absolutely new, no matter what our past sins or experiences.

The implication of this in terms of God's goal for our lives is that we are not any longer trying to become 'holy'. We are already holy. We are not trying to become pleasing to God. We are already pleasing to him.

It is important to note at this point that if you try to live out your Christian life without understanding just what you already have, just what a fantastic foundation has been laid, you will simply be 'trying harder', in effect trying to obey a set of rules. The glorious freedom that Jesus has given us liberates us from that law concept. Once we know who we are in Christ, who God is and the truth that we are new creations, we won't be 'acting like we think Christians should act', as one person put it to me. We will be living out the truth of our new identity. We won't be working for God's approval or for our salvation. We'll be working to show our love and gratitude to him. If we have not resolved those things, the rest of this book may depress us, because it will seem like a list of things we have to try harder to do. As always, freedom does not come from trying harder. It comes from knowing the truth. If you find yourself slipping back into a 'trying harder' mentality, you may want to revisit the earlier books in the series.

We have escaped the corruption in the world

The original Greek makes it clear that this escape from the corruption in the world is something that has already happened: literally it would read, 'having escaped the corruption in the world caused by evil desires'.

Peter assures us that we have indeed escaped the corruption in the world. We no longer have to give in to sin. We can choose every day to walk by the Spirit rather than according to the desires that come from our flesh. In short, we are free – free to choose, just as Adam and Eve were before they sinned.

So let's be clear about one thing. Working out what God's overriding goal for our life is and then fulfilling it has nothing to do with becoming acceptable to God. If you are a Christian, you are already pleasing to him. Deep down inside you are now very nice. It has nothing to do with working *for* your salvation. It's about working *out* your salvation. The starting point is the amazing change that took place in you the moment you became a Christian.

There is nothing more you need in order to set about fulfilling God's goal for you. You already have everything required.

If you have been working through the first three books in the series, you will have a greater appreciation of just what it means to be 'in Christ'. If you have taken the opportunity to go through The Steps To Freedom In Christ as recommended in the third book, you will have cleared out any 'rubbish' getting in the way of moving on and you will understand the importance of continually renewing your mind by making a determined choice every day to throw out ways of thinking that are not in line with God's Word and choosing to believe the truth, whether it feels true or not.

Once you know the truth about yourself, God and Satan, understand the nature of the battle you are in against the world, the devil and the flesh, and have resolved issues from the past, the blue touchpaper has been lit. You are ready to explode into fruitfulness!

It really is for freedom that Christ has set you free (Galatians 5:1). You can make a genuine choice to walk in that freedom and become the person God created you to be. Nothing and no one can stop you.

The goal

The passage goes on to show us God's goal for our lives:

> *For this very reason, make every effort to add to your faith goodness; and to goodness, knowledge; and to knowledge, self-control; and to self-control, perseverance; and to perseverance, godliness; and to godliness, brotherly kindness; and to brotherly kindness, love. For if you possess these qualities in increasing measure, they will keep you from being ineffective and unproductive in your knowledge of our Lord Jesus Christ. But if anyone does not have them, he is nearsighted and blind, and has forgotten that he has been cleansed from his past sins. Therefore, my brothers, be all the more eager to make your calling and election sure. For if you do these things, you will never fall.* (2 PETER 1:5–10)

Did you spot a goal in there that meets all the criteria we outlined earlier? Possibly not. However, look again. Peter wants us to start with faith. Faith is simply bringing our belief system into line with what is already true. It's seeing things as they really are, the way God tells us they are in his Word. Faith has always been the starting point in life as a Christian. It's not a mystical force that suddenly comes upon us – really it's a firm determination, a choice, to act according to God's Word rather than according to the deception that the world, the flesh and the devil throw at us.

So it starts with faith. We are then to make every effort to build on our faith and add to it a number of qualities: goodness, knowledge, self-control, perseverance, godliness, brotherly kindness, and love.

What we have here is a list of *character* attributes. This is where we begin to understand God's goal for our lives. His primary concern is not so much what we *do* but what we're *like*. His goal for us is to do with our character.

Looking at the list, you may notice that 'knowledge' stands out at first glance as something that appears not to be a character attribute. However, balance that with this statement from Paul:

> *Knowledge puffs up, but love builds up. The man who thinks he knows something does not yet know as he ought to know. But the man who loves God is known by God.* (1 CORINTHIANS 8:1–3)

We need to make a distinction between different types of knowledge. Paul says that a goal of having knowledge for its own sake will lead to pride, a character attribute that is the opposite of what God wants us to be like. Anyone who makes this a goal 'does not yet know as he ought to know'. The sort of knowledge that Peter wants us to aim at is a knowledge that speaks of knowing a person intimately, a knowledge that comes from having a character moulded and changed by God.

So God's goal for our life is to do with what we are like, with seeing our character move from where it is now to a higher level. Ultimately, the goal is for us to become like Jesus.

You can see the same goal outlined throughout the New Testament. For example:

> *Now the Lord is the Spirit, and where the Spirit of the Lord is, there is freedom. And we, who with unveiled faces all reflect the Lord's glory, are being transformed into his likeness with ever-increasing glory, which comes from the Lord, who is the Spirit.* (2 CORINTHIANS 3:17–18)

The goal that God has for any Christian, then, could be defined as follows: to become more and more like Jesus in character. The great news is that nobody and nothing on earth can keep you from being the person God planned. Except, of course, you!

On the other hand, Christians who are not committed to God's goals for character tend to fall. According to Peter, they have forgotten that they have been cleansed from past sins (2 Peter 1:9). In other words, they forget who they are in Christ. If you have forgotten who you are in Christ, what's the best thing to do? Remember!

Does this goal meet the criteria that we laid out earlier? Let's check.

Measurable

Peter promises that as these character qualities increase in your life through practice, you will be useful and fruitful, and you will never fall. Wow! Quite apart from being a fantastic basis for a true sense of worth and success, this also demonstrates that the increase in character qualities is something that can be discerned, something that can be measured through the fruit you bear.

Achievable

We noted earlier that God would not ask us to do something that we could not do – that would not be fair. Is the goal to adopt Jesus' character attributes genuinely achievable? Well, it will be the work of a lifetime and none of us will ever have characters that completely reflect his. However, all of us have the opportunity to see our characters move from the level where they are now to a higher level, to show progress. In other words, all of us can achieve the goal of becoming more and more like Jesus in character.

Not dependent on other people

Can other people stop you growing in these character attributes?

I have come across a number of people who feel that their spouse is holding them back from really fruitful ministry, perhaps because the spouse is not a Christian, or maybe just doesn't see things the same way, so is not supportive. I have seen people at their wits' end because they feel that their lack of ability to engage in the ministry they want prevents them from fulfilling God's goal for their lives. If only their husband or wife would see things as they do and join with them in serving the Lord, they think, then everything would be OK.

Behind that thought, however, is the notion that God's goal for their life is to do with ministry, with what they *do*. It is not. That is not what God is measuring.

> *The Lord does not look at the things man looks at. Man looks at the outward appearance, but the Lord looks at the heart.*
>
> (1 SAMUEL 16:7)

Yes, other people can get in the way of what you do for the Lord. But they cannot get in the way of what you are *like*. Think of the patience and perseverance that you could develop as you face this situation, choose to love and honour your spouse and put their needs before your own. And patience and perseverance are the very things the Lord is interested in!

What could we say to a husband who is in this situation? How about something like this: 'I will help you persevere in this situation to become the person God wants you to be. You can't change her, but you can change yourself, which may be the best way to influence her anyway. Even if she does not change, you can come through this with your character having become more like Jesus, which is a great basis for hope.'

Don't get me wrong – I'm not saying that he is at fault. He may rightly ask, 'What if the problem is 90 per cent hers?' He doesn't have any control over that. He can't change her. By committing to change *himself* he is dealing responsibly with what he *can* control. His transformation may be just the motivation his wife needs to change herself. Whether or not that happens, however, God can use those difficult circumstances to help him move further along towards his goal of becoming more like Jesus.

Not dependent on circumstances

You may think that your past or present circumstances are so difficult that they stop you becoming the person God wants you to be. Paul teaches, however, that the difficulties we face, far from getting in our way, are actually a means of achieving our supreme goal of becoming more like Jesus:

> *We rejoice in our sufferings, because we know that suffering produces perseverance; perseverance, character; and character, hope. And hope does not disappoint us, because God has poured out his love into our hearts by the Holy Spirit, whom he has given us.* (ROMANS 5:3–5)

James offered similar advice:

> *Consider it pure joy, my brothers, whenever you face trials of many kinds, because you know that the testing of your faith*

develops perseverance. Perseverance must finish its work so that you may be mature and complete, not lacking anything.

(JAMES 1:2–4)

Persevering through difficulties results in an improved character. God's goal for our life is to do with our character – what we are like – rather than with what we do.

Defeated spouses say, 'My marriage is hopeless,' then try to 'solve' the problem by changing partners. Others feel their jobs or churches are hopeless. So they move, only to discover that their new job or church is just as hopeless. What should you do? Hang on in there and use the situation to develop your character. Those difficult situations may well be helping you achieve God's goals for your life. There are legitimate times to change jobs or churches, but if we are just running from our own immaturity, it will follow us wherever we go. In fact, I have often noticed in my life that if I run away from a particular situation instead of persevering through it and developing my character, God in his grace usually confronts me with an almost identical situation a little later. If I run away from that one, he gives me another... and another... until I learn the lesson that he wants me to learn.

Is there an easier way to become more like Jesus other than enduring difficult situations? We have all looked for one, but it is usually the difficult times of testing that bring about the maturity that makes life meaningful. We need occasional mountain-top experiences, but the fertile soil for growth is always down in the valleys, not on the mountain-tops.

Not dependent on how gifted we are

You may have thought that your lack of talents, intelligence or other gifts prevents you from being as successful or happy as other Christians in your walk with the Lord. Yet there is no mention in Peter's list of talents, intelligence or gifts. The fact is that these things are not equally distributed to all believers:

some have one talent, others have ten. 'That's not fair! How can God do that?' you might ask. Because your identity and sense of worth are not determined by those qualities. Your sense of worth is based on two things: who you are in Christ; and your growth in character.

Every Christian is able to see their character grow from where it is now to a higher level. Every Christian is able to become more like Jesus. God's measure is absolutely fair. Although gifts and opportunities are not distributed equally, it is equally possible for a Christian with ten talents and a Christian with just one talent to demonstrate growth in character.

When we get to heaven, I suspect we will be surprised to see just who receives the various rewards and places of honour. It will not necessarily be those with the most visible ministries in this life.

The character of Jesus

As Peter lists the character attributes we are to aim at, he adds one to another to another until he arrives at the final one: love.

This is no accident. After all, God *is* love (1 John 4:8). If you wanted one word to sum up the character of Jesus, 'love' would be it.

Let's look at the classic passage on love, often read at weddings, and see what light it sheds on our goal:

> *If I speak in the tongues of men and of angels, but have not love, I am only a resounding gong or a clanging cymbal. If I have the gift of prophecy and can fathom all mysteries and all knowledge, and if I have a faith that can move mountains, but have not love, I am nothing. If I give all I possess to the poor and surrender my body to the flames, but have not love, I gain nothing.* (1 CORINTHIANS 13:1–3)

Can you see now why Paul says that things we do that might look incredibly impressive gain us precisely nothing if we have no character development to go with them? You may have a wonderful-looking ministry, you may do all sorts of impressive things for God. But if your character is not becoming more like Jesus', it does not impress God. It counts for nothing in the light of eternity because God is not measuring what you do but what you are like.

> *Love is patient, love is kind. It does not envy, it does not boast, it is not proud. It is not rude, it is not self-seeking, it is not easily angered, it keeps no record of wrongs. Love does not delight in evil but rejoices with the truth. It always protects, always trusts, always hopes, always perseveres.*
>
> (1 CORINTHIANS 13:4–7)

In a very real sense, love encapsulates all of the other positive character attributes that God wants us to develop.

> *Love never fails. But where there are prophecies, they will cease; where there are tongues, they will be stilled; where there is knowledge, it will pass away. For we know in part and we prophesy in part, but when perfection comes, the imperfect disappears.* (1 CORINTHIANS 13:8–10)

Things we *do* will pass away. The effects of love, however, last for eternity.

Doing versus being

Some may be feeling a little uncomfortable with this emphasis on what we are *like* rather than what we *do*. Doesn't that mean that we can just sit around doing nothing, waiting for the Lord to return?

Well, we could. But that would not be the mark of a character that is becoming more like Jesus. His life was marked by extended times of prayer and extended times of 'doing'. He spent himself on behalf of those who needed him. Having a character of love, how could he not?

The big issue here is what we believe makes us pleasing to God and brings glory to him. Is it our character (what is inside) or is it what we do (what is outside)?

In Mark 7:14–15 Jesus made a statement that his disciples found hard to understand:

> *Listen to me, everyone, and understand this. Nothing outside a man can make him 'unclean' by going into him. Rather, it is what comes out of a man that makes him 'unclean'.*

When they were alone Jesus spoke further to them about this (verses 17–20):

> *Don't you see that nothing that enters a man from the outside can make him 'unclean'? For it doesn't go into his heart but into his stomach, and then out of his body... What comes out of a man is what makes him 'unclean'. For from within, out of men's hearts, come evil thoughts, sexual immorality, theft, murder, adultery, greed, malice, deceit, lewdness, envy, slander, arrogance and folly. All these evils come from inside and make a man 'unclean'.*

The principle here is that it is what is on the inside that leads to external actions, good or bad. If we try to shortcut this and just try to conform externally to a set of rules, we end up with mere religion. God looks at the heart, what is on the inside. Jesus was saying that we should not kid ourselves into thinking that some ritual makes us clean if our heart is in a bad state. God will see straight through it. But if our heart is good (and you have been given a brand-new heart!), it will lead to good actions.

So it's not that we don't do good things. It's all about the motivation. If we think we need to do good things in order to please God or prove ourselves to others, we'll be constantly agitated, often close to burnout. If, on the other hand, we concentrate on our character, becoming more like Jesus, we will increasingly act like he did.

You cannot become more like Jesus inside and not have at least some of his compassion. That will lead you to want to spend yourself on behalf of others as he did. You cannot become more like Jesus inside and not have at least some sense of his justice. That will lead you to stand up for those who cannot stand up for themselves. You cannot become more like Jesus inside and not want to tell others how they can find him too.

We'll choose to love the unlovely. We'll want to serve. Indeed, ultimately we will want to become like him even in his sufferings and death (Philippians 3:10).

Applying God's Goal to the Whole of Life

In July 2007 at the Keswick Convention, the great Bible teacher, Dr John Stott, gave what he said would be his last public address at the age of 87. There was great interest in what topic he would choose. He started by posing this question: 'I remember very vividly, some years ago, that the question which perplexed me as a younger Christian (and some of my friends as well) was this: what is God's purpose for His people?' His conclusion? 'I want to share with you where my mind has come to rest as I approach the end of my pilgrimage on earth and it is – God wants His people to become like Christ. Christlikeness is the will of God for the people of God.'[1]

When we adopt the goal of becoming more and more like Jesus in character, we will want to make sure it flows through into the whole of our lives. Any other goal we adopt needs to sit below that and not conflict with it.

The problem is that, whether we realize it or not, we have for many years been living with different goals. As we grew up, our thinking was shaped by the world system we lived under, which promised to meet our deep needs for significance, security and acceptance, needs which were God-given and which can only be completely fulfilled in him. We developed goals to meet these needs, but independently of God.

We may not even realize that we have been working towards other goals, but, once our basic needs for physical survival are met, we all have a driving need to feel good about ourselves. It's what the world calls self-esteem. In practice, people will say simply that they want to be 'happy' – happiness comes when they feel good about themselves, when their needs for significance, security and acceptance are being fulfilled.

But what if the things you think will bring you happiness actually turn out to do the opposite?

I've never considered myself much of a do-it-yourself expert but in recent years I've discovered that I can actually 'do it myself' and get a reasonable result. I've now laid wooden floors in most of the downstairs rooms in our home. Some are better than others, I have to say. I'm naturally very much of the 'Oh, that will do' mentality. I tend not to take great pains to get the details right but press on in the hope that it will all work out in the end. I have discovered, however, through painful experience, that with wooden floors, if you don't take a lot of effort to ensure that you are laying the first few rows of wooden blocks in a straight line, it usually doesn't work out. You get into trouble later on. The first few rows look OK but gradually, as rows are added, the original misalignment is magnified so that halfway into a room, you start to see quite large cracks between the wooden blocks.

Our dining-room floor has quite a few cracks between the pieces of wood which get bigger the further away you get from the starting point. Thankfully, it's a relatively small room so there is not that much space for the cracks to become catastrophic. They are not quite big enough for a small dog to fall through, for example! I'm proud to say, however, that our living room, on the other hand, doesn't have any cracks at all. That's because I learned the importance of getting the first few rows absolutely straight while I was doing the dining room. The additional time that it took to do that paid for itself many times over – trying to compensate as best I could for the cracks in the smaller room took an inordinate amount of time.

It's like that in the Christian life. As we start out, the things we have come to believe will make us happy (when we were simply following the line the world fed us) will not be in line with what will actually make us happy as revealed by God in the Bible. Thankfully, God does not expect us to be instantly mature. It's not disastrous at that stage. But if we continue to live that same way for many years, cracks will eventually start to appear and our life as Christians, which is meant to be the most fulfilling thing imaginable, may seem far from fulfilled and our effectiveness in playing our part in God's plan will be dented.

I'm in my mid forties and coming to terms with the fact that I'm middle aged. In the last five to ten years I have been shocked to see how many people of my age have encountered what might be termed mid-life crises. My children are in the minority at school in coming from a home where both parents are still together. I've seen church leaders burn out and leave the ministry. Christians I know have turned to adultery, with disastrous results for their families. Many have devoted themselves to developing a career, only to find that the success they were looking for and later received did not bring the satisfaction they thought it would. I've gone down my fair share of dead ends too, of course. I've discovered that living on adrenaline can only be maintained for so long; that working frenetically leads to burnout; that looking to other people for approval leads to compromise. Most of the wrong turns and bad decisions that people take seem like the right thing at the time. But they don't lead to the expected conclusion – happiness and fulfilment – because they are not in line with truth.

The longer we persist in believing the wrong things, the less fulfilling and productive our lives will be. As we play 'the next nine holes' of our lives, if we want to do well, we will need to make sure that we iron out anything in our belief system that is not in line with truth, and adopt goals that are in line with God's overall goal for us, to become more and more like his Son in character.

We will want to work out what goals we still have that are not compatible with God's goals for us, and to throw them out by changing our thinking, and then wholeheartedly adopt God's goals for our lives.

It might be helpful at this point to define exactly what we mean by 'goals'. All of us spend our lives working for the things that we have come to believe will make us happy and fulfilled. These are our goals. I am specifically referring to those outcomes we have come to believe are fundamental to our sense of who we are and what we achieve in our lives, those results by which we measure our very selves. It is possible, of course, to have other objectives – such as reading the rest of this book by next Saturday, getting to work on time every day or staying awake during the talk at church – but if we fail to achieve them, we will probably just shrug our shoulders and resolve to try harder in future. In this book, the term 'goal' does not include those things. It is about the big things we have come to believe are fundamental to our sense of fulfilment and achievement in life which, if we don't achieve them, leave us feeling inadequate or thinking we are failures.

What are your specific goals? Often we are unable to say – perhaps not even to ourselves – because we have simply set off on a course that we have learned to believe will make us happy, without giving it a great deal of thought. I suspect that you, like me, are simply not aware of all your unconscious goals, but it is important to become aware of them so that you can see whether they fit under God's overall goal for your life of making you more and more like Jesus in character.

We ask participants in the Freedom In Christ Discipleship Course a series of questions in order to help them work out what their goals are. Please spend a few minutes looking at these. Rate yourself from 1 (very low) to 5 (very high) on each one and answer the 'I would be more' question.

1. How successful am I?   1 2 3 4 5
   I would be more successful if...

2. How significant am I?   1 2 3 4 5
   I would be more significant if...

3. How fulfilled am I?   1 2 3 4 5
   I would be more fulfilled if...

4. How satisfied am I?   1 2 3 4 5
   I would be more satisfied if...

5. How happy am I?   1 2 3 4 5
   I would be happier if...

6. How much fun am I having?   1 2 3 4 5
   I would have more fun if...

7. How secure am I?   1 2 3 4 5
   I would be more secure if...

8. How peaceful am I?   1 2 3 4 5
   I would have more peace if...

I'd be fascinated to know what you put there. I wonder if any reader has scored themselves a 5 on every question. In fact, do you think it could be right for a Christian to score a 5 on every question?

Well, does God want you to be successful? Does he want you to feel secure? One thing's for sure. He certainly hasn't called you to be a miserable, unfulfilled, insignificant failure! We can all hope to get to the point where we can put 5s in answer to those questions, if not all the time then most of the time. Of course, it comes down to what we mean by 'successful', 'significant' and so on. If you feel a little uncomfortable about working towards a 5, you may well not have the same definition for 'successful', 'significant' and so on as God has. Consequently, you may not be living up to your God-given potential and you may be in danger of taking some wrong turns. The key to staying on the right path is understanding the truth about what success, significance and so on really are and how they tie in with our overriding goal of becoming more like Jesus.

We will look shortly at each of the areas covered by the questions to see how we can make our goals in each area compatible with God's overriding goal for our life. First, however, let me introduce you to three fictitious people.

The first is a church leader called James who really wants to fulfil his calling as leader to the glory of God. Recently, he has been surprised and a little concerned at how angry he has been. He's found himself losing his temper with his family and his leadership team.

The second is a parent called Chris with two teenage children who, although they still come to church, are obviously there under duress. Chris has been seen as a wonderful parent but has recently started suffering from panic attacks (I've deliberately chosen a name, incidentally, that could be applied either to a mum or a dad!).

The third is a lovely single lady called Sarah who is always a regular at church. She is bouncy, enthusiastic and popular. At least historically she has been. In recent years it has looked as if the bounce has all but disappeared and it's rare to see her smile.

Let's assume that all of them accept the principle that the overriding goal God has for their lives is that they should become more and more like Jesus in character. How should they carry that through into setting goals for other areas of their life? Most likely they simply haven't thought about it that much and are simply working towards goals that seem good to them.

Let's look at James, our church leader, first. He is passionate about seeing people become Christians. He believes that Christians can transform the communities they live in through the life and love of Jesus. What would be a good goal for him in his ministry as a church leader? If you ask him, he is very definite. His goal, he says, is to reach his community for Christ. Is that a good goal?

We looked earlier at certain characteristics that apply to God's goals for our lives. Any God-given goal will be: measurable; achievable; not dependent on other people; not dependent on circumstances; and not dependent on how gifted we are.

Two of these characteristics in particular will help us evaluate whether our goals are God-given or not: looking at whether they are dependent on other people or circumstances that are outside our control. Who can get in the way of James' goal to reach the community for Christ? Every member of the community for a start (oh, and a couple of the members of his leadership team!).

James arrived in the church three years ago full of passion and enthusiasm, with well-thought-out plans to train his people to reach out to their neighbours and friends. He put his heart into excellent training and equipping programmes. There has been some success. A steady trickle of new Christians have come into the church and are integrating well. But it is at a far lower level than James envisaged and he senses that the church is tiring a little of his constant attempts to get them to engage with non-Christians.

If he were to complete the questions we looked at earlier, he might rate his success at around a 2 out of 5 and would say something like, 'I would be more successful if the rate of new Christians tripled.' His satisfaction would be at a similar level and he might say, 'I would be more satisfied if my leadership team would really get behind the vision for reaching the community.' As for fun and peace, they would probably merit a big fat zero!

The issue is that James' goal, the outcome he uses to assess his whole sense of success in his calling as church leader, is dependent on other people over whom he has no control. He can use all his considerable skills of motivation and persuasion but ultimately the outcome is not in his hands. His sense of fulfilment is like a plastic cup being carried away by a torrent of water after heavy rain. He has no idea where it will end up.

Emotional signs

I mentioned that James has been concerned about how angry he has been recently. His normal temperament is calm but he has become increasingly frustrated with the members of his church who do not seem to share his passion for reaching the community. He has been surprised at the angry outbursts he has with his close family and his anger has been boiling over into his sermons too. They have become increasingly condemnatory in nature. In fact some people have stopped coming, saying they feel bad enough already without being condemned by the pastor when they come to church.

We saw in the third book in the series just how important our emotions are. They are the system God has given us to alert us to areas of our belief system that are out of line with truth. If we are heading towards a goal that is not in line with God's goal for us, again our emotions perform the highly useful role of alerting us to this, just as James's anger is.

I saw a sign on a door which said 'This Door Is Alarmed'. I'm not sure what had alarmed it but it didn't seem to be getting any better – poor thing! I remember another sign that said 'Beware: This Building Is Alarmed'.

James justifies the harder line taken in his messages by the ultimate outcome: seeing the community won for Christ. However, he may as well be wearing a sign around his neck saying 'This Pastor Is Angry'. When a goal we have is consistently blocked, it results in anger.

We saw earlier that no God-given goal can be dependent on other people or circumstances outside our control, so we can conclude that no God-given goal can be blocked. If, therefore, you have a goal that is being blocked, it is not a God-given one. James' anger, then, is pointing out to him loud and clear that he is currently working towards a goal that, good though it seems, is not in line with God's goal for him.

Is it wrong for him to want to see the community reached

for Jesus? Of course not. Jesus told us to go into all the world and make disciples. The problem comes when he uses this as a measure of his own self-worth or success in ministry.

What would be a better goal for James? Well, let's remember that our overriding goal, to become more and more like Jesus, is primarily concerned with what we are *like* rather than what we *do*. It is about our character.

What if he were simply to adopt the goal of being the best possible leader he can be – that is to say, to be the most Christ-like leader he possibly can be? That is a goal based on character. Nothing and no one can prevent him achieving it – except himself!

The function of a leader is to 'prepare God's people for works of service' (Ephesians 4:12). Where will these works of service take place? Well, mostly out in the world, in their jobs and neighbourhoods. As James changes his goal and simply works towards being the best possible leader, he will stop seeing his people as a means to accomplish *his* goal of reaching the community for Christ and instead will be genuinely concerned to help them understand and accomplish God's goals for *their* lives. Instead of using condemnation to inspire guilt to get them to 'try harder', he will help them understand God's grace and just what it means to be in Christ.

Many of us in church leadership, if we are honest, are trying to rope our people into helping us meet the goals we have for *our* ministry instead of helping them to fulfil *their* ministry, which is our real function.

When James changes his goal and aims at becoming the best possible pastor, his people notice an immediate change. They begin to feel much more secure and valued for who they are. They no longer feel that they have to perform in a certain way to get his approval. From this base of knowing their security in Christ and knowing security in their relationship with James, they will find they want to reach out to the community as the love of Christ grows in them.

You can see the same principle working in Paul's letters to the churches he was responsible for. He spends the first half of every letter simply reminding them of who they are in Christ and what they already have in him. Only in the second half of the letter, when he is sure they have understood this, does he move on to telling them how to behave. God wants our work for him to come from a sense of security and affirmation rather than a sense of condemnation – we work for him not because we have to but because we want to.

Paradoxically, giving up the people-dependent goal of reaching the community for Christ in favour of a character goal may well result in the original goal being accomplished anyway!

Anger highlights a blocked goal

Some emotional honesty will help us enormously. Like the sign on that alarmed door, maybe it would help for Christians to wear little emotional signs around their necks so that, despite their fixed smiles and assurances of 'I'm very well!' on Sundays, we might see what's really going on: 'This Christian Is Angry', 'This Christian Is Anxious' or 'This Christian Is Depressed'. Possibly also perhaps 'This Christian Is Alarmed'!

If James can look honestly at these feelings of anger, they can prompt him to examine what he has been believing, see that it's not quite in line with truth, and make the necessary adjustments. His feelings of anger are pointing out to him that someone or something has got in the way of his goal. Something or somebody is preventing him from accomplishing what he wanted.

If you don't want to be angry, get rid of any goal that can be blocked by other people or circumstances that you have no right or ability to control.

Whenever you feel angry, try to work out what goal is being blocked. I don't know about you, but I have a strange knack of always choosing the wrong queue in the supermar-

ket. No matter how short the queue, a problem develops...
The anger that sometimes rises up is because my goal to get
through the checkout quickly in order to be somewhere else
has been blocked. What I may not realize is that God may be
deliberately causing that to happen in order to help me grow
in the godly virtue of patience.

'What, God deliberately makes life difficult? I thought
he was supposed to work in all things for my good!' you may
retort. Have a look at what Paul actually says in context:

> And we know that in all things God works for the good of those
> who love him, who have been called according to his purpose.
> For those God foreknew he also predestined to be conformed
> to the likeness of his Son, that he might be the firstborn among
> many brothers. (ROMANS 8:28–29)

Yes, he is indeed working in all things for your good because
you are among those who have been called according to his
purpose. Which is? To be conformed to the likeness of his Son
– to become more and more like Jesus in character!

Sometimes that may well mean that in his wisdom God
can see that I will benefit from struggling in difficult circumstances, that this will help me move further towards reaching
my goal. Instead of getting angry, I can rejoice in an opportunity to move towards the overriding goal of my life, which is to
become more and more like Christ in character.

Anxiety highlights an uncertain goal

It's not just anger that shows up faulty goals. Another emotion,
anxiety, does too. To demonstrate that, let's have a look at
another of our fictitious characters. Chris is the parent of two
teenage children who, although they still come to church, are
obviously there under duress.

What would be a good goal for a Christian parent? Chris
simply wants to have a loving, happy Christian family with

everyone going on well with the Lord. Well, that certainly sounds like a good goal. However, it may well lead to anger because it's likely to be blocked rather frequently. Who can block it? Every person in the family not only can but will!

The teenagers are good, loving kids at heart and have benefited from growing up in a secure Christian family but, as they find their own identity, they are beginning to resent the lack of choice that Chris is giving them regarding church. They are not sure they want to be Christians – at least they want to know they have made their own decision. They are beginning to rebel. Chris senses that time is running out and that they cannot be forced to continue coming to church for much longer. In any case, it is embarrassingly obvious to other church members, from the long faces and body language, that they don't want to be there. Yet Chris's goal is to have a loving, happy Christian family and is measuring personal success by that.

Chris prays and prays for a breakthrough, and buys all the latest Christian teen magazines in the hope that they will be read and will lead to a change of heart. Instead it becomes more and more obvious that one day soon the teenagers will put their foot down and turn their back on their parents' faith. Yet Chris clings onto the hope that a breakthrough will come as they listen sullenly to the message on Sunday or sit tight-lipped through the worship.

Chris has rightly been seen by others as a wonderful parent but has recently started suffering from panic attacks. The problem is that Chris is measuring success as a parent by the achievement (or not) of having a family full of Christians who are going on with the Lord, but is not in a position to make that happen – it is a goal that is dependent on other people. Chris's whole sense of value as a parent is therefore in the hands of other people. That is not healthy.

That is not to say that seeing our family move on with the Lord is not something that we should aspire to – it is, and we should do everything within our power to make it happen. But if we're going to measure our score on the last nine holes by how other people behave, we're setting ourselves up for some problems. A parent who believes that their sense of worth is dependent on how their family behaves will fall apart every time their spouse or children fail to live up to their image of family harmony. Their sense of worth ends up being totally dependent on the actions of other people.

As well as the anger caused by a blocked goal, Chris feels anxious much of the time. Anxiety comes when we do not know what will happen. Chris hopes that the children will come through but does not know whether or not they will.

If Chris had completed the questionnaire we looked at earlier, we would probably see a low score for 'happiness' and something like, 'I would feel more happy if the children made definite commitments to Christ.'

When you feel anxious in a task or a relationship, it's an emotional sign that achieving your goal feels uncertain. You are hoping something will happen, but you have no guarantee that it will. You can control some of the factors, but not all of them.

For example, if you have come to believe that your sense of worth or well-being depends on financial success, you will probably suffer from anxiety. Why? Because you have no guarantee that you can ever get enough money or, even if you feel you have enough, that it won't be wiped out by a stock-market crash or some similar occurrence.

If we want to get rid of anxiety, we need to get rid of goals that are uncertain, because no God-given goal for our lives need be uncertain. God has given us everything we need to live a godly life (2 Peter 1:3).

So what would be a good goal for Chris? How about 'to be the parent God wants me to be'? This is a character goal in line with the overall goal of becoming more and more like Jesus. Adopting that goal may well end up having a positive effect on the children because when you cooperate with God, you can expect your life to bear good fruit.

God – the perfect parent

Parenting is the most significant task that many of us will undertake. It is so easy for us to value our whole sense of achievement and self-worth by how our children perform or to impose unhelpful expectations on them. If you are a parent and you believe that your sense of worth depends on how your children turn out – perhaps your goal is for them to become missionaries, doctors, lawyers or pastors – it can put you on a collision course with them.

As your children reach their teenage years, their behaviour will not always match your ideal. They want their freedom but you feel that you've got to control their behaviour because you believe your success as a parent depends on how they turn out. If they don't attend the functions you want them to attend, they can't go anywhere. If they don't listen to the music you expect them to listen to, they lose their TV rights.

In fact, parenting is an eighteen-year process of letting go. The fruit of the Spirit is not child-control but self-control (Galatians 5:23).

Being a parent is tough. I have found it immensely helpful simply to try to follow the example of God, who is the perfect parent. Of course, it helps to have a clear idea in our own mind of what God is really like. If we see him as an authoritarian fig-ure, a kind of heavenly headmaster looking for us to put a foot wrong, this doesn't really work. However, if we connect with the truth that he is love, that we are already accepted, that he does not ever make us do anything we do not ourselves choose to do, then it works very well. It enables us to create a frame-work for our own children whereby they know that, although we will discipline them from time to time, it's for their own good, and nothing they can do can make us love them more or love them less: they are simply accepted. They will know that we will support them to the utmost in their life but that they are free to make their own choices.

It came as a revelation to me when my children were very

young that God simply loves me no matter what I do, that his love is not based on my behaviour but on his character – he is love and he cannot do anything but love. I determined to act the same way towards my children and, from an early age, have assured them that nothing they can do will ever change the fact that I will love them. They have always liked to act a series of 'What if' questions such as 'What if I murder someone?' or 'What if I take drugs?' and have been assured that my love for them will not change. I remember the first time that my younger daughter got a serious telling-off and was sent to her room as part of the discipline process. She looked at me through her tear-stained eyes and said, 'Dad, you still love me just as much, don't you?' 'Yes,' I responded. She smiled. She was secure even in the midst of discipline.

The risk you take is that your children will say, 'Well, I'll just behave any way I want to, then.' In practice that rarely happens, just as it doesn't happen when we discover that our heavenly Father's love for us is not based on our behaviour. In fact, it makes them want to please us more, not to gain our approval but simply because they want to.

We parents need to know that our own sense of self-worth is dependent simply on who we are in Christ and the growth in our character to become more like Christ. It has nothing to do with how our children behave. We will want to do our best to bring them up in the way of Christ and to discipline them when they go wrong, but at the end of the day they are their own people and will make their own choices.

Depression highlights an impossible goal

Sometimes an uncertain goal seems to slip even further away to the point where its fulfilment begins to appear impossible. You feel, 'It's never going to happen.' That is what has happened to Sarah, our lovely single lady who used to be the bouncy, enthusiastic one at church but who in recent years has become more and more withdrawn and depressed.

Ever since she was a little girl Sarah has looked forward to the day when she can get married and go on eventually to have children. She has somehow felt that being a wife and mum would happen and, without her realizing it, achieving that has become fundamental to her sense of self-worth.

She has probably never vocalized the fact that having a husband and children are her 'goal', but if she had completed the questionnaire we looked at earlier, she would almost certainly have scored herself very low on 'fulfilment' and would have said something like, 'I would be more fulfilled if I could just find a husband and settle down', a good indication that this desire has attained the status of a 'goal' to her.

She has prayed and waited over the years but somehow the right man has never come along. She has been through anger with God and anxiety about a future on her own. Now she is slipping into depression as she starts to believe that the goal will never be fulfilled.

When you base your future success on something that you come to realize can never happen, you have an impossible, hopeless goal. Your depression is an emotional sign that your goal, no matter how spiritual or noble, may never be reached. Depression can also be caused by biochemical reasons, of course, but if there is no physical cause, then it is often rooted in a sense of hopelessness or helplessness.

I've known people whose whole sense of success as a Christian seems to depend on a loved one coming to the Lord, often a husband. They pray for them, witness to them, invite them to event after event. They say everything they can say and do everything they can do. If they are not careful, they may find that the whole issue can seem as if it's more about fulfilling a need they have within themselves than genuine concern for the other person's eternal destiny. Sometimes nothing works and as their efforts seem more and more futile, their faith falters and they end up falling into depression as their goal begins to seem impossible. That, of course, in itself can make their goal less likely to be achieved.

It is, of course, right to want your loved ones to come to Christ, and to pray and work to that end. But when you base your sense of worth as a spouse, parent or friend on the salvation of your loved ones, you set yourself up for some problems. Why? Because their response is beyond your ability or right to control. All we can do is share our faith in the power of the Holy Spirit and pray. The results are in the hands of God and the other person. We can't save anyone.

Sarah's depression shows that she is desperately clinging to a goal that she believes she has little or no chance of achieving, and that's not a healthy goal.

What would be a good goal for Sarah to adopt? She could look at where God has planted her in the family of her local church and adopt the goal of 'being the best possible friend and church member'. She in no way needs to get rid of her desire for a husband and family and can keep asking God for that, but she needs to know that she is already complete in Christ and that fulfilling her potential here on this earth has nothing to do with having a husband and children. She can make a decision to leave the future in God's hands, knowing that, whatever happens, there is nothing to stop her becoming the person God wants her to be. Her sense of worth comes from who she is in Christ and the growth in her character to become more and more like Jesus.

Realizing the truth of that and knowing that no Christian is helpless or hopeless will probably be a key to helping Sarah recover from her depression.

Wrong goals lead to manipulation and control

The problem with goals that can be blocked by other people or circumstances beyond our control is that they lead us to try to manipulate the people and circumstances that need to be changed in order for them to be fulfilled.

For example, a pastor's goal might be to have the finest youth ministry in the area. However, one of his leadership team attempts to block that goal by insisting that a worship ministry is more important. Every attempt by the pastor to take on a youth pastor is vetoed by the influential leader who wants to take on a full-time worship leader first. The pastor believes that his sense of worth and success in ministry is on the line.

So he tries to push the stumbling block out of the way. He lobbies his cause with other members of the leadership team. He solicits support from denominational leaders. He preaches on the importance of youth ministry to gain congregational support. He looks for a way to change his opponent's mind or remove him from the team, because he believes (wrongly) that his success as a pastor is dependent on reaching his goal of having a great youth ministry.

The result is likely to be division. If, on the other hand, his goal had been character-based, he could have used the disagreement with the other leader to humble himself, and develop patience.

It is not hard to understand why people try to manipulate circumstances or control others. They believe that their sense of worth is dependent on other people and circumstances. But that is not true. This is amply demonstrated by the fact that manipulators and controllers are amongst the most insecure people you will ever meet.

The difference between a 'goal' and a 'desire'

There's a good chance that you might be feeling a little confused right now. I've given examples of things that seem good to work towards – like reaching a community for Christ, seeing a husband become a Christian or having a family where every member is moving on with the Lord – and said that these are not good goals because their outcome is not under your control.

That does not mean that you should not pray and work for these things with all your heart! What it means is that you should bear in mind that their outcome is not within your power or ability to determine, and therefore you should not in any sense use the outcome as a measure of your own success or failure as a Christian or as a person. In other words, these outcomes are not the measure God is using as he looks at the success of your Christian life. At the end of your life, when you stand before him, he will not ask you why your child did not become a missionary, why your husband did not become a Christian, why you did not get married or why a particular member of the community turned their back on him. He may well ask *them* those things, but he will not ask you because those things are not your responsibility.

What do we do with a goal whose fulfilment is in itself a good thing but which depends on events or circumstances that we cannot control? We certainly do not need to abandon it. We do, however, need to downgrade it in our thinking from a goal upon which our whole sense of who we are depends, to what Neil Anderson calls 'a godly desire'.

The crucial difference is this: what we are calling a *godly goal* is a specific calling from God that reflects his overall purpose for your life to become more like Jesus in character, but does not depend on people or circumstances beyond your ability or right to control; a *godly desire*, on the other hand, is a specific result that *does* depend on the cooperation of other people, the success of events or favourable circumstances which you have no right or ability to control.

Whom do we have the ability and right to control? Only ourselves. The only person who can block a godly goal or make it uncertain or impossible is you.

The crucial difference is that you cannot base your success or sense of worth on your desires, no matter how godly they may be, because you cannot control their fulfilment.

We will struggle with anger, anxiety and depression when

we elevate a desire to a goal. But by contrast, when a desire isn't met, all that happens is that we will face disappointment. Life is full of disappointments and we all have to learn to live with them. However, dealing with the disappointments of unmet desires is a lot easier than dealing with the anger, anxiety and depression of goals which are based on wrong beliefs. When you begin to align your goals with God's goals and your desires with God's desires, you will rid your life of a lot of anger, anxiety and depression.

Chris, the parent we met earlier, may go along with the suggestion that being the best possible parent is a good goal but may object, 'What if my spouse has a mid-life crisis or my children rebel?' Problems like that are not blocking the goal of being the best possible parent. In fact, if ever the children and spouse need Chris to be the best possible parent, it's at times like that!

A pastor whose success and sense of worth are based on his goal to win his community for Christ, have the best youth ministry in the area or increase giving by 50 per cent, is heading for a fall. These are worthwhile desires, but no pastor should deem himself a success or failure based on whether or not they are achieved. No member of his church or community, however, can block the goal of being the most Christ-like pastor possible. Even the difficulties of members who complain, vandals who wreck church property and leaders who have strong (and different) opinions simply provide opportunities for him to work towards becoming more like Jesus.

Please do not get hung up on the terminology I am using – 'goals' and 'desires' – but do understand the principle. One church leader, having taken this teaching to heart, asked this eminently sensible question on Freedom In Christ's online forum:

> Many churches set goals each year, for anything from financial turnover to evangelistic projects to starting new

groups, etc. Is it wrong to set such goals (perhaps they are 'aims')? Talking about 'church desires' for the year sounds a lot weaker!

Frankly, it does not matter whether you still refer to things whose outcome is outside your ability to control as 'goals', as long as internally you are secure in the knowledge that whatever the outcome is, it does not reflect on your value or on how God measures your success in the Christian life.

Goals and desires may seem only subtly different but understanding the distinction between them can make a huge difference to the way you work out your Christian life. If you make godly character your primary goal, then the fruit of the Spirit that will be produced in your life is love, joy (instead of depression), peace (instead of anxiety) and patience (instead of anger).

Going for straight 5s

I discovered a fascinating grave at a church near my home. It belongs to one Powlett Wrighte. There is a long inscription about him which ends as follows:

He died at Bristol whither he went for the recovery of his health 22nd July 1779 aged 40 years.

Oh dear, poor Powlett. The curative qualities of Bristol obviously did not live up to the brochure hype. His goal was blocked in a decisive way!

As we mentioned earlier, we need to remember the fact that we are going to die. One day you will lose everything you have, including your closest relationships, your qualifications, your possessions and your money.

There is just one thing you will not lose. That is your

relationship with Jesus and everything that comes with it. But that's far better than everything else. For a Christian, death is not the end but a wonderful beginning.

That is why Paul can say, 'For to me, to live is Christ and to die is gain' (Philippians 1:21). However, if you try putting anything else other than Christ in that verse, it doesn't work. For me, to live is my career, to die is… loss. For me, to live is my family, to die is… loss. For me, to live is a successful Christian ministry, to die is… loss. But when the point of our life here and now is simply Christ and becoming like him, when we die it just gets better.

Earlier, I asked whether it would be right for a Christian to respond with straight 5s (the top mark) to the questions beginning with 'How successful am I?' on page 36.

Let's now look at the areas in those questions in the light of the overarching goal God has for us to become more and more like Jesus in character, so that we can adopt goals in these areas that are compatible with it.

Success
Does God want you to be successful?

> *Blessed is the man who does not walk in the counsel of the wicked or stand in the way of sinners or sit in the seat of mockers. But his delight is in the law of the Lord, and on his law he meditates day and night. He is like a tree planted by streams of water, which yields its fruit in season and whose leaf does not wither. Whatever he does prospers.* (PSALM 1:1-3)

Make no mistake. God wants you to be successful and prosper in everything you do. He wants you to be fruitful. And, according to this passage, if you live according to how God says things are, that is what will happen. The big question, however, is what does that mean?

'Success' means different things to different people at

different times. In New Testament times, for example, in the culture that Paul the Apostle was brought up in, it meant having a good religious pedigree, being ultra-religious and demonstrating religious zeal. Using that definition of success, Paul was a highly successful person. He had everything going for him. However, when he discovered what God meant by success, he said this:

> *But whatever was to my profit I now consider loss for the sake of Christ. What is more, I consider everything a loss compared to the surpassing greatness of knowing Christ Jesus my Lord.*
> (PHILIPPIANS 3:7–8)

What does 'success' mean in our culture? I looked it up in a dictionary[2] and found two interesting definitions:

- The favourable outcome of something attempted.
- The attainment of wealth, fame etc.

The first definition is the generally accepted one – achieving what you set out to accomplish; achieving your goals.

The second definition is more illuminating in terms of our own culture. It specifically identifies wealth and fame as the goals that need to be attained. These are so commonly sought that they are now virtually incorporated into the very meaning of the word 'success'. The definition might equally have read, 'the attainment of a humble, loving character' if that were the main concern of our culture. But in our culture success has come to mean wealth and fame, as illustrated by the famous saying of Paul Getty that success is easy to achieve – you just need to get up early every morning, work hard... and strike oil!

That second definition of success, however, does not agree with God's definition of what it means to be successful. As we have seen, the goal God is measuring us against is how much our character becomes like Jesus' character. It has nothing to do with what we have or what people think of us but everything to do with what we are like.

When God says that he wants us to be successful and to prosper, it does not mean that he wants us to be rich and famous! It means that he wants us to attain the goal he has for us and for us to be fruitful in his terms.

If you want to see a list of people whom God judges to be successful, you could do no better than to turn to Hebrews 11. This chapter contains a list of people from the Old Testament who are there by virtue of their success in God's eyes.

Interestingly, it does contain people who were rich and who enjoyed great fame and wealth: Moses; Joseph; David; Abraham. These people certainly fit our culture's definition of success, so success in God's eyes is not necessarily incompatible with worldly success.

But we also find others in the list: Noah, who was ignored by his countrymen; and Rahab, who was a prostitute. And we find that some of the people listed are considered successful despite the fact that they did not live blameless lives: David, for example, committed murder and adultery; Moses committed murder.

What do these examples have in common? The writer to the Hebrews says it was simply this: they all lived by faith in God. Faith is much more than belief. It can be defined as taking God at his word (see Hebrews 11:1) or, as in a previous book in this series, seeing things as they really are (i.e. as God says they are) and living accordingly.

Real faith is demonstrated by actions. Successful Christians in God's eyes are ones who base real-life decisions on what the Word of God says when the world tells them to do something else. When Joshua led Israel into the Promised Land, God said to him:

> *Be strong and very courageous. Be careful to obey all the law my servant Moses gave you; do not turn from it to the right or*

*to the left, that you may be successful wherever you go. Do not
let this Book of the Law depart from your mouth; meditate on
it day and night, so that you may be careful to do everything
written in it. Then you will be prosperous and successful.*

(JOSHUA 1:7–8)

Was Joshua's success dependent on other people or favourable
circumstances? No, success hinged entirely on one thing: If
Joshua believed what God said and did what God told him to
do, he would succeed. Sounds simple enough, but God immediately put Joshua to the test by giving him a rather unortho-
dox battle plan for conquering Jericho. March around the city
for seven days, then blow a horn. Imagine trying to sell that to
your military planners!

But that's what God told him to do. Joshua's success had
nothing to do with the circumstances of the battle and everything to do with obedience.

Look back at how you answered this question earlier.
What did you say after 'I would be more successful if…'? That
probably will help you understand what 'success' has come to
mean to you. If you wrote something like 'I could show more
of Christ's love', your definition of success is in line with God's.
If you wrote 'had a better job', 'earned more money', 'had more
spiritual gifts' or anything to do with other people or circumstances you cannot control, you may want to do some work on
how you understand success to bring it into line with God's
view.

Success is accepting God's goal for our lives and by his
grace becoming what he has called us to be. If you want to
be successful, make sure your goal is the same as God's goal
for you – seeing your character become more like Jesus' – and
make that your top priority.

For a dozen years or so I have been running a small
mail-order business. It enabled Freedom In Christ Ministries
to get started in the UK by providing office space, some free

labour and an infrastructure. Yet it has rarely turned in a profit and seems to have followed something of a hand-to-mouth existence. In contrast, Freedom In Christ Ministries has grown significantly and seen what you might call 'success' (depending on what definition you are using!), and most of my time is now spent on the ministry rather than the business. Learning that the business is hard grind most of the time and does not even make money, whereas the ministry seems to have been granted a great deal of blessing, many have asked (not unreasonably) why I do not simply close the business and concentrate fully on the ministry.

I could give many reasons – a reluctance to make staff redundant, a hope that it will all come good or whatever – but the bottom line is that, every time I have asked him, the Lord has made it clear that the business should carry on. Not only that, he has shown me that in his eyes my work for the business is just as important as my work in the ministry. How can selling a toy be compared to seeing someone's life change as they get hold of key truths from God's Word? Well, it can't. However, that is not the measure God is using.

I have come to realize that the whole point of the business and the difficulties I have experienced in it is to develop my character. I know – and God knows even better – that I am prone to pride. Although on the one hand I know that any 'success' the ministry has seen is not down to me but down to God, I seem to be adept at somehow falling into patterns of thinking that attribute it to me! I know for sure that if, over the last several years, I had simply experienced the 'success' of the ministry without the difficulties in the business, I would be completely insufferable (as it is, I'm only somewhat insufferable!).

When creditors are pressing and I have no idea how to pay the bills, I have often prayed for the Lord to change the circumstances. Paul did something of the same when he faced a difficult situation:

To keep me from becoming conceited because of these surpassingly great revelations, there was given me a thorn in my flesh, a messenger of Satan, to torment me. Three times I pleaded with the Lord to take it away from me. But he said to me, 'My grace is sufficient for you, for my power is made perfect in weakness.' Therefore I will boast all the more gladly about my weaknesses, so that Christ's power may rest on me. That is why, for Christ's sake, I delight in weaknesses, in insults, in hardships, in persecutions, in difficulties. For when I am weak, then I am strong.   (2 CORINTHIANS 12:7–10)

For me, difficulties in the business have functioned exactly like the 'thorn in the flesh' that Paul talks about. The whole point of God sending it to him was character development: to stop him becoming conceited because of the great things God was doing.

When you start to get God's orientation on life and bring your goal in line with his goal for your life, then you really can welcome hardships and difficult circumstances because they will further your chances of attaining success in God's eyes by reaching your goal of becoming more like Jesus.

I would much rather be a success according to God's terms and a failure in the eyes of the world than a success in this world but a complete failure for all eternity.

In the last few weeks three people on three separate occasions have referred to me as 'humble'. Each time that has happened, I have struggled because I know better than anyone else what is lurking below the surface and how prone I am to be proud, how easily I can slip into taking credit for what God has done (and I recognize the danger in writing this paragraph). Yet I also know that a decade ago just about everyone who knew me saw my pride. Jesus has done a remarkable thing in helping me turn away from measuring my success in human achievements (career, ministry, financial or whatever) and measure it instead in Christlikeness. I still have a very long way to go. The point, however, is that there has been a change, one that has been noticed by others. That gives me great encouragement. And I know that it is Christ himself who has made it possible by giving me difficult circumstances to cope with. I really do know now that difficulties are to be welcomed – far from blocking my goal, they can be used to make me more like Christ, something that will last for eternity.

Significance

How did you score yourself on significance? Let's see whether your understanding of significance is in line with God's.

When we passed from the twentieth century to the twenty-first, I remember seeing a plethora of TV programmes and newspaper articles looking at the most significant moments, songs, people, novels, inventions, revolutions, disasters or whatever from the twentieth century and usually ranking them. I noticed that in many of these, there seemed to be a disproportionate number of entries from the most recent decades. I wondered how different the list would be if compiled by reviewers fifty years or so later, when there would be an opportunity to have a better sense of perspective.

In 1917 a French artist called Marcel Duchamp surprised the art world by entering a porcelain urinal in a New York art exhibition, unchanged since it left the manufacturers apart from the name 'R. Mutt' scrawled on it. He called it *Fountain* and declared that it was art simply because he said so. Perhaps even more surprising to many, in 2004 a committee of British art experts voted it the most influential piece of modern art of the twentieth century, ahead of works from the likes of Picasso and Matisse. Part of me wants to scream, 'That's ridiculous!' but another part of me recognizes that if the impact that *Fountain* made was still recognized by so many nearly ninety years on, then it was genuinely significant.

Significance is about time. What is forgotten in time is of little significance. What is remembered for eternity is of great significance.

The tragedy is that we may not realize our own significance. I have two memories that I can date clearly to the year 1969 when I was seven years old. On 1 January my mother gave birth to a healthy baby girl of nine pounds. She had been due before Christmas but held out to the New Year. I remember the doctor saying, 'Only a year late!' and myself being sent around the neighbourhood to tell friends the good news. On 20 July that same year my parents made me stay up well beyond my bedtime to watch fuzzy pictures on the TV: live coverage of the first moon landing. I remember begging to be allowed to go to bed and my father replying, 'You will be able to tell your grandchildren that you watched it as it was happening.' So far I have told my children (who didn't seem terribly impressed!) but I look forward to telling my grandchildren in due course.

Which of those events was more significant? The first was just a baby being born – it happens all over the world all the time. Well, she thought it was significant! So did I. I bet you can't even name all of the astronauts who landed on the moon. I wonder how much God cares about moon landings. I know he cares deeply about people.

It's easy to feel that we are not significant. Look what God said when his people thought that they were so insignificant, that he had forgotten them:

> *But Zion said, 'The Lord has forsaken me, the Lord has forgotten me.'*
> *'Can a mother forget the baby at her breast and have no compassion on the child she has borne? Though she may forget, I will not forget you! See, I have engraved you on the palms of my hands; your walls are ever before me.* (ISAIAH 49:14–16)

He uses a graphic illustration – engraving us on the palms of his hands. In other words, he has put us somewhere where we will never be forgotten. No matter how much time passes, we will still be there. That makes us hugely significant!

When it comes to the question of time, Christians know that our life is about much more than our 'three score years and ten'. We are not just looking at our life on earth but at the whole of eternity. Yet what we do during our earthly life influences eternity. How can we make sure that our earthly lives are significant?

When 'the Day' comes and our work is tested by fire, what are the types of activity that will survive? Which are genuinely significant? Those with consequences that last for eternity.

You may say, 'All I do is help with the children at church.' Wow, you are teaching truth to five-year-olds! What they choose to believe will have eternal consequences. That makes it very significant indeed, quite apart from the significant service you are performing for their parents in freeing them to worship God and learn about him.

I used to work for the largest computer company in the world doing advertising and promotion, and I looked after a budget that ran into eight figures... I thought I was doing some pretty significant things commissioning advertising campaigns that ran on the TV and so on. Who remembers those ads now? Just me! But what happens in heaven when just one sinner repents? They all throw a party! There are no insignificant children of God, and there are no insignificant tasks in the Kingdom of God.

You are significant simply because you are you. Jesus would have died for you if you had been the only person ever who needed him to do that. If you want to increase the significance of what you do over 'the next nine holes', focus your energies on significant activities: those that will remain for eternity.

Fulfilment

Everybody wants to be fulfilled. There is so much in newspapers, magazines and self-help books about it. Yet not that many people actually seem to be fulfilled!

Jesus must have been the most fulfilled person that ever

walked the earth. Where did he get his sense of fulfilment from? 'My food is to do the will of him who sent me and to finish his work' (John 4:34). Interestingly, it didn't come from trying to be fulfilled. It came when he focused not on himself but on serving God the Father.

Peter wrote: 'Each one should use whatever gift he has received to serve others, faithfully administering God's grace in its various forms' (1 Peter 4:10). God has made each one of us unique. We have different gifts. Yet we are to use them to serve others – and when we do, paradoxically, we will be fulfilled.

I am privileged to meet with church and ministry leaders for prayer once a week in the city where I live. We are consciously demonstrating our unity and praying for the city. Every week when we get there just before 8 a.m., a light breakfast has been laid out together with tea and coffee. The other week I asked Dennis, who serves it to us, what he had done to draw the short straw of being the guy in his church who has to get there early to do that rather thankless task. His reply surprised me. Apparently he is not employed by the church but is an ordinary member of it. He considers the meeting of leaders to be so important that he has volunteered to be there every week. Not only does he provide for our needs but he tells me that once the meeting is underway, he stays around and prays for us and then tidies up afterwards. Wow!

Contrary to what the world would have us believe, fulfilment has very little to do with our external circumstances. Fulfilment comes when we 'grow where we're planted' rather than believing that we need to change some circumstance or person in our lives.

God has a unique place of ministry for each of us. The key is to discover the roles we occupy in which we cannot be replaced, and then decide to be the person God wants us to be in those roles. For example, of the 6 billion people in the world, I'm the only one who can be married to Zoë Goss (at least, no one else had better try!) or who can be father to my two lovely daughters. You have a unique role as husband, father, wife, mother, parent or child in your family – no one can be that person better than you. God has specially planted you to serve him by serving your family.

You have been placed in unique friendship relationships too. You are the only one who knows your neighbours as you do. You occupy a unique role as an ambassador for Christ where you work. These are your mission fields and you are the worker God has appointed for the harvest there. Your greatest fulfilment will come from accepting and occupying God's unique place for you to the best of your ability and looking for ways to meet the needs of those around you.

The paradox is that so many people are desperately trying to be fulfilled. Fulfilment comes, not when we specifically try to find it, but when we use our unique gifts to serve God and other people.

Don't try to be someone else. Be the unique person that God has made you to be. On 'the Day' God won't ask me why I wasn't Billy Graham – but he might ask me why I wasn't me!

Satisfaction

How did you rate yourself on your level of satisfaction? I wonder what you thought would make you more satisfied – again a clue as to what you have come to believe will bring satisfaction. Jesus said, 'Blessed are those who hunger and thirst for righteousness, for they shall be filled [i.e. satisfied]' (Matthew 5:6). If you wrote something like, 'I would be more satisfied if I worked harder for righteousness in my community', you are on the right lines.

As our characters become more and more like Jesus, we will find ourselves hungering and thirsting after righteousness. Our hearts will break at injustice. We will want to walk in the light in the whole of our lives.

The truth is that nothing else really satisfies except living a righteous life. If you think that is too hard, you should try living a sinful life – that's when things really do get difficult!

Can you think of an experience with a tradesperson or a shop that left you dissatisfied? What was the issue? It is generally to do with quality: that is to say, the quality of service or of a product. We become dissatisfied when the quality goes down.

Satisfaction is about quality, not quantity. We achieve greater satisfaction from doing a few things well than from doing many things in a haphazard or hasty way. The key to personal satisfaction is not found in doing more things but in deepening commitment to quality in the things that we are already doing.

The same is true in relationships. If you are dissatisfied in your relationships, perhaps you have spread yourself too thin. Solomon wrote: 'A man of many companions may come to ruin, but there is a friend who sticks closer than a brother' (Proverbs 18:24). Satisfaction comes from having a few quality friends who are committed to meaningful relationships with one another. We need a couple of deep relationships.

That's what Jesus modelled for us. He taught thousands and he equipped seventy for ministry, but he invested most of his time in twelve disciples. Out of those twelve, he selected three – Peter, James and John – to be with him at crucial times: on the Mount of Transfiguration, on the Mount of Olives and in the Garden of Gethsemane. The result was shown while he was suffering on the cross. He was able to commit the care of his mother to John. That's a quality relationship. We all need the satisfaction that quality relationships bring.

So satisfaction will come when we commit to living righteously and seek to raise the level of quality in our relationships and in everything we do.

Happiness

There has never before been a society like ours, in which people have so many things yet are so unhappy. Why? Because things do not make us happy! What I find strange is that you would be hard-pressed to find anyone who disagrees with that statement, yet practically everyone seems to live as if it were not true. When there is a mismatch between what people say they believe and what they do, their actions always show what they really believe.

The world's concept of happiness is having what we want. Advertisements tell us that we need a flashier car, a more expensive perfume or any number of items that are better, faster or easier to use than what we already have. We watch TV commercials and read ads, and we become restless and start to want all the latest fashions and gadgets. We are deceived into thinking we can't be really happy until we have what we want. Paul wrote:

> *Godliness with contentment is great gain. For we brought nothing into the world, and we can take nothing out of it. But if we have food and clothing, we will be content with that.*
>
> (1 TIMOTHY 6:6–8)

This is the exact opposite of what the world is constantly telling us. According to Paul, true happiness is not having what we want but wanting what we have. All the time we focus on what we don't have, we will be unhappy. But when we begin to appreciate what we already have, we'll always be happy.

What do we have? Everything we need to live a godly life (2 Peter 1:3), every spiritual blessing (Ephesians 1:3), Christ himself, eternal life, the love of a heavenly Father who has promised to supply all our needs (Philippians 4:19). No wonder the Bible repeatedly commands us to be thankful (1 Thessalonians 5:18), especially when you consider what we actually deserve: hell! If you really want to be happy, learn to be content with life and thankful for what you already have in Christ.

Yet we are tempted continually to say, 'I want more!' God brought the Israelites out of slavery, gave them clear guidance as to where to go (a pillar of cloud by day and a pillar of fire by night), and provided regular food for them. What did they say? 'I want more!' They complained about everything, even saying that they would prefer to be back in slavery.

In the West we are used to having an enormous choice of things to buy, whether it's food in the supermarket or items for our home. We set increasingly high standards for the organizations we buy from, wanting 24-hour availability, speedy delivery and so on. It's easy to take this consumer mentality into church. I've lost count of the number of Christians I've known who have moved church because the old one 'wasn't meeting my needs'.

Church isn't there to meet your needs. You are part of church so that you can meet the needs of others and glorify God! Paradoxically, as you do that, you will yourself be enriched.

When we get to heaven and God asks us how our life was, will we say, 'It was OK but I would have liked a bit more'? When he says, 'I gave you my only Son', will we say again, 'But I wanted more'?

Happy are those who want what they have.

Fun

You may think fun is a strange thing to include in this list. Yet of all people, a Christian who has been set free by Christ, and knows who they are and what they have in him, should be having fun!

Have you ever planned a major fun event? Some years ago I decided to give my wife a birthday surprise. I gave it a big build-up, telling her we needed to get up early and travel 100 miles. It was a lovely hot day and we set off. She didn't know where we were going. By the time we arrived some hours later at our destination – Stratford-Upon-Avon – she had it in her mind that we were going hot-air ballooning or on a river cruise. She wasn't expecting to spend three hours inside a dark theatre watching a Shakespearean tragedy, even if it was the wonderful Royal Shakespeare Company. She assured me she enjoyed it but there was more than a slight sense of let-down.

Often when you plan for fun, it leads to a let-down because it doesn't turn out as expected. The chances are that the last time you really had fun, it happened spontaneously. Maybe it was a pillow fight with the kids or a ridiculous conversation with a friend – it just happened.

Fun happens when we are able to throw off our inhibitions. That is why so many people get drunk when they go out socializing. They know they need to get rid of their inhibitions and alcohol helps them do that – though, of course, it has a plethora of unhelpful side effects.

Children of God do not need to get drunk in order to have fun. The secret to enjoying uninhibited spontaneity as a Christian is to remove unbiblical hindrances.

When David got the Ark of the Covenant back, which had been stolen by the Philistines, he was so happy that he leaped and danced before the Lord in celebration. His wife, Michal, was embarrassed by his behaviour, much as my children are when they see me dancing at a disco. She thought his behaviour was unbecoming to a king, and she told him so in no uncertain terms. David said, 'I will celebrate before the Lord. I will become even more undignified than this' (2 Samuel 6:21–22). As it turned out, Michal was the person God judged in the incident, not David (verse 23). Which provides great encouragement for all you other disco-dancing dads out there – just be yourselves!

The main thing that gets in the way of Christian fun is our tendency to keep up appearances. We don't want to look out of place or be thought less of by others, so we stifle our spontaneity with a form of false decorum. That comes from the flesh and amounts to 'people-pleasing'. Paul wrote, 'If I were still trying to please men, I would not be a servant of Christ' (Galatians 1:10).

Do you still find yourself thinking, 'What will people say?' Those walking in freedom will respond, 'Who cares what people say? I'm not playing to the crowd any longer. I'm playing for God alone.' It is a lot more fun pleasing the Lord than trying to please people.

I have always been someone with more inhibitions than most. When I have thrown them off, it has certainly made life more fun. It has also enabled people to see the real me, just as they were always able to see the real Jesus.

I have realized that the same embarrassment that keeps me from having fun also keeps me from telling others about Jesus, if I do not make a constant effort to throw it off. It's still very much a work in progress for me, but in terms of a goal for my life, I'm determined to become more like Jesus in the way that he lived as a 'what-you-see-is-what-you-get', genuinely whole person.

A lot of funny things happen in church. I remember one Christmas, one of the leaders at my old church addressed the congregation surrounded by Christmas decorations and candles. He inadvertently knocked over one of the candles, which set fire to some paper. It was at this point that he noticed the fire that was starting to take hold. Instead of stopping and turning his attention to it, he carried on talking as if nothing had happened while trying to put the flames out surreptitiously with his notes... which caught fire! One of the other leaders stepped in and dealt with the small blaze. The speaker continued without batting an eyelid as if nothing whatsoever had happened. Why? It was hilarious to those of us who were watching, yet he somehow felt that because it was church he could not acknowledge the reality of the situation but simply had to press on.

When my father-in-law died, I had the privilege of doing the address at his funeral service. I started by telling his favourite joke. I was intrigued to see the looks on people's faces, especially those who were not regular churchgoers. They were (not unreasonably) expecting seriousness and 'religion'. There was quite a pause before they realized it was OK to laugh in church.

How have we managed to give people the impression that our wonderful, loving, creative God is a killjoy?

When we are free, we can laugh. We don't need to keep up appearances.

Security

'I would be more secure if...' Actually, the truth is that a Christian cannot be more secure than they already are. Jesus said that no one can snatch us out of his hand (John 10:27–29). Paul declared that nothing can separate us from the love of God in Christ (Romans 8:35–39) and that we are sealed 'in him' by the Holy Spirit (Ephesians 1:13–14). How much more secure can you get than that?

We can, however, feel insecure when we depend upon earthly things that we have no right or ability to control. It's all too easy to fall into the trap of working towards a goal of finding our security in money or some other worldly thing. In fact, if our security is anywhere other than God, it would be impossible not to feel insecure because it cannot be guaranteed.

Our world is in trouble and there are some tough times ahead. The population is exploding and natural resources are decreasing. What will happen when the oil runs out? And that's without even thinking about climate change, terrorism or the threat of nuclear war. It's likely that events in the world will shake us and show us where our security really lies.

Although it's difficult to be optimistic about the future of the world, I'm very optimistic about the future of the church, incidentally. As we shall see later, we have every hope of reaching this generation for Christ and seeing our towns and cities turned upside down for him.

We can only find real security in one place: in the eternal life of Christ. Every 'thing' we now have, we shall some day lose. Jim Elliot, a missionary who was murdered, said, 'He is no fool to give up that which he cannot keep in order to gain that which he cannot lose.'

I have decided that my security is in Christ. My goal is to become ever more certain of the truth that nothing can take me out of his hand, and live accordingly.

Peace

My mother attends a church which has a bell-tower but no bells. The neighbourhood does, however, resound to the sound of bells from the tower every Sunday morning – they come from an amplification system in the tower. At one time my mother was in charge of starting the 'bells' on a Sunday morning, which involved getting an old-fashioned record player going. Unfortunately, the record of the bells was a little scratched so the sound that echoed over the neighbourhood was far from perfect.

She was attending a concert and happened to notice that one of the performances was given by a church choir from the South of England. She recognized the name of the church from the record that she had to put on every Sunday and sought out a member of the choir and got into conversation. The result was that the lady from the choir offered to record a round of bells from her church especially for my mother's church if my mother would send her an audio cassette. The cassette was duly despatched and returned with the 'live' recording. My mother's church happily threw away the ageing record player and invested in a cassette player. On the first Sunday that the new system was used, all went well for the first twenty minutes or so. The peaceful sound of bells rang out over the neighbourhood. There was then a brief pause before the neighbours were rudely jolted out of their peaceful state of mind by the sound of nursery rhymes being broadcast loudly from the tower! The tape my mother had sent had previously been used to record some songs for her grandchildren.

Actually, the peace of God has nothing to do with what is going on outside. It is internal, not external; it's to do with what's going on inside you rather than with circumstances outside.

Because of the sacrifice Jesus made in our place, Christians already have peace *with* God (Romans 5:1). The peace *of* God, however, is something that we need to take hold of every day in our inner person. And we can have it even in the midst of storms that rage in the external world. This is Jesus' promise to us:

> *My peace I give you. I do not give as the world gives. Do not let your hearts be troubled and do not be afraid.* (JOHN 14:27)

A lot of things may disrupt our external world because we can't control all of our circumstances and relationships. But we can control the inner world of our thoughts and emotions by allowing the peace of God to rule in our hearts on a daily basis. There may be chaos all around us, but God is bigger than any storm. That is why Jesus puts the onus on us – 'Do not let your hearts be troubled' – as does Paul:

> *Let the peace of Christ rule in your hearts, since as members of one body you were called to peace.* (COLOSSIANS 3:15)

Jesus is the Prince of Peace (Isaiah 9:6), but it is our responsibility to let his peace rule in our hearts. How?

> *Do not be anxious about anything, but in everything, by prayer and petition, with thanksgiving, present your requests to God. And the peace of God, which transcends all understanding, will guard your hearts and your minds in Christ Jesus.*
>
> (PHILIPPIANS 4:6–7)

For this area of our lives, then, we might aim always to bring our requests to God with thanksgiving and then leave them with him. That is a goal that would be consistent with the way Jesus acted and would result in the peace of God guarding our hearts and minds.

NOTES

1. www.langhampartnership.org/
2. *Collins English Dictionary.*

God's Goal for You as Part of the Body

So, God's overriding goal for you and me is for us to become more and more like Jesus in character. And the character of Jesus is love.

Despite the impression often given of them, the Pharisees were generally sincere people who wanted to do what was right. They tended to go wrong in their understanding of what would please God in that they thought it was down to behaving in a certain way. At one point they wanted to test Jesus and they asked him which was the greatest commandment that God had given to his people. In Matthew 22:37–40 Jesus gave his response:

> 'Love the Lord your God with all your heart and with all your soul and with all your mind.' This is the first and greatest commandment. And the second is like it: 'Love your neighbour as yourself.' All the Law and the Prophets hang on these two commandments.

Yet again we find that what pleases God is love, a character attribute. Genuine love will result in loving actions, but it starts deep down inside with a character that is like God's own.

Jesus shows us here that our love should have two objects: firstly God, and then those around us. We all have an individual relationship with God. But we also have relationships with those around us. If the goal God has for us is love, then that love is to be expressed both towards him and towards others.

Being the you God planned involves more than just being

in a righteous relationship with him. It involves those around you too. In fact, you cannot become more and more like Jesus in isolation. Nowhere will our character be seen more clearly than in how we relate to others.

'We love because he first loved us' (1 John 4:19). We give freely because we have received freely (Matthew 10:8). We are merciful because he has been merciful to us (Luke 6:36), and we forgive in the same way that Jesus has forgiven us (Ephesians 4:32). If you have taken hold of your freedom in Christ, you are free to relate to others as God intended.

So we now turn our attention to understanding how to relate to others – even people who really get up our nose! – and why the main thing Jesus chose to pray for those who would come after his disciples (that's you and me) was that we would be one (John 17:20–23). Functioning as part of the body of Christ is a key part of being the person God wants us to be.

We'll look first at some biblical principles about relating to others on an individual basis. Then we'll go on to see why this is so crucial when it comes to fulfilling God's goal for the whole of his church.

Relating to others

Our rights and responsibilities

In any relationship, we have both rights and responsibilities. It's important to understand what these are and where we should put the emphasis.

We have the right to be respected regardless of skin colour, nationality, gender, age and so on. However, we have no right (or responsibility) to judge anyone else:

> *Who are you to judge someone else's servant? To his own master he stands or falls. And he will stand, for the Lord is able to make him stand.* (ROMANS 14:4)

Judgment is an issue of character which, as we have seen, is fundamental to God's goal for our lives. Someone else's character is simply none of our business – it is an issue between them and God. We are not to judge them by expressing an opinion about their character. Each person is responsible before God for their own character. We do, on the other hand, have responsibilities to others:

> *Do nothing out of selfish ambition or vain conceit, but in humility consider others better than yourselves. Each of you should look not only to your own interests, but also to the interests of others. Your attitude should be the same as that of Christ Jesus...* (PHILIPPIANS 2:3–5)

Where we do have a responsibility before God for other people, it is to meet their needs. We are to look not only to our own interests but also to the interests of others, and our attitude towards them is to be like that of Jesus himself – something that will become more and more natural, the more our character takes on his attributes.

Our responsibilities can be summed up as: developing our own character and meeting the needs of others. This is not what comes to us naturally, to say the least! There's something in me that so wants to be able to point out other people's character faults to them and to explain why *they* should be meeting *my* needs.

The question is, where should we put the emphasis – on our responsibilities or on our rights? Take a Christian marriage, for example. It is true that the Bible tells wives to submit to their husbands, and a husband might focus on that as his right. But a husband is also given a corresponding responsibility: to love his wife as Christ loved the church (and just think what that means). Which should he emphasize: his right or his responsibility?

A wife may nag her husband because she thinks she has a

right to expect him to be the spiritual head of the household. It's true that he has been given that calling by God. She, on the other hand, has been given a responsibility to love and respect her husband. Where should she put the emphasis – on her right or on her responsibility?

Again, it is helpful to look at this in the light of 'the Day'. When we stand before Christ, where will he put the emphasis? Will he ask us whether those around us gave us everything they should have, or will he focus on how well we fulfilled our responsibilities? He will reward us for how well we fulfilled them. Satan, on the other hand, will always tempt us to focus on our rights rather than on our responsibilities.

Yes, we have rights in every relationship we are in. But we also have a responsibility to love one another, to care for one another, to accept one another and to encourage one another. We are each to focus on our own responsibilities.

I have had to tread much more carefully at home since my children discovered this verse: 'Fathers, do not exasperate your children; instead, bring them up in the training and instruction of the Lord' (Ephesians 6:4). They seem to dust it down and bring it out at every opportunity – strangely, however, they only seem to quote the first part!

Do parents have a right to expect their children to be obedient? Or do they have a responsibility to bring them up in the training and instruction of the Lord, and discipline them when they are disobedient? They have both, of course – where they put the emphasis is the critical issue. Those who emphasize their rights are likely to be heading towards being overbearing disciplinarians. Those who emphasize their responsibilities are likely to be far more like Christ.

Does being a member of a local church give you the right to criticize others? Or does it give you a responsibility to submit to those in authority over you and relate to one another with the same love and acceptance we have received from Christ? As we shall see later, being a member of a local church is an incredible privilege that comes with an awesome responsibility.

Of course, we do all have rights. Everybody has a right to be loved and accepted irrespective of race, colour or creed, but we must not abdicate our personal responsibilities by demanding our rights.

I learned a long time ago not to expect anything from anyone else. It takes a lot of stress out of relationships if I simply focus on doing my part. But, of course, others often do go out of their way to meet my needs – when that happens, because I wasn't expecting it, it's a wonderful bonus.

Learning not to focus constantly on the failings of others and choosing to think well of them is so much easier in the long run than always feeling let down and badly treated.

What about when others do wrong?

It's all very well saying that we are to focus on our own character and responsibilities and think well of others. But what about when they do things that are clearly wrong? Are we simply to pretend they didn't happen?

It's important to realize right up front that there is not a person on the planet who finds it easy to own up to sin. Most of us do eventually get to the point where we are honest about our failings, but it can take a struggle and we may well choose to open up only in front of certain people where we feel secure.

That's a very important thing to bear in mind when it comes to looking at whether we should alert other people to their failings. The truth is that we can often see what the issues are in someone else's life much more clearly than they can. But is it our responsibility to be the conscience of another person and persuade them of their sin which, as we have seen, is a task that is far from easy? No, that is the role of the Holy Spirit (see John 16:8).

You can be sure that the Holy Spirit is already gently convicting them of their sin or character failing. They are already undergoing something of an internal battle with him. The moment we try to intervene and point out the sin, we become the focus of the struggle that they are supposed to be having with God. And we are not up to it.

What, leave it to the Holy Spirit to tell them their failings? Yes. We have been given a ministry of reconciliation, not a ministry of condemnation. Love does not *expose* a multitude of sins – it *covers* them (1 Peter 4:8)!

I have learned that when I seem to be constantly wanting to criticize others and point out their faults, I need to take a long hard look at the state of my own relationship with the Lord. In Isaiah 6:1 we read:

> *In the year that King Uzziah died, I saw the Lord seated on a throne, high and exalted, and the train of his robe filled the temple.*

Isaiah had an amazing experience of God. What was the result?

> *'Woe to me! I am ruined!' I cried. 'For I am a man of unclean lips, and I live among a people of unclean lips, and my eyes have seen the King, the Lord Almighty.'*

If we, like Isaiah, saw God in his glory, whose sin would we immediately become aware of? Someone else's? No, our own!

In Luke 5 Jesus appropriated Peter's boat to speak to the crowd who had gathered. Peter had been fishing all night without success. Jesus said to him, 'Put out into deep water, and let down the nets for a catch.' Although he probably couldn't see the point, Peter obeyed. He went back to the lake and started pulling in fish after fish. This was a genuine miracle. He must have suddenly realized that Jesus was no ordinary man. What was the result? He became aware of his own sin and blurted out, 'Go away from me Lord; I am a sinful man!'

When we see God for who he is, we become aware not of

the sin of others, but of our own sin. However, when we are lukewarm in our relationship with God, we tend to overlook our own sin and see the sin of others. As we have seen, however, our responsibility is not for their character but for our own character. Their character is a matter between them and God.

Habakkuk 3:17–18 has always been one of my favourite passages:

> *Though the fig tree does not bud and there are no grapes on the vines, though the olive crop fails and the fields produce no food, though there are no sheep in the pen and no cattle in the stalls, yet I will rejoice in the Lord, I will be joyful in God my Saviour.*

When I was a teenager I used to quote this Bible reference in Christmas cards that I sent to other young people in my church group. My handwriting has never been a strong point and a lot of young people have never heard of a book of the Bible called 'Habakkuk'. So, I now know, my scrawled 'Hab. 3:17–18' was usually read as 'Heb. 3:17–18' – slightly but significantly different! Anyone who bothered looking up the passage they thought I was referring to would find this:

> *And with whom was he angry for forty years? Was it not with those who sinned, whose bodies fell in the desert? And to whom did God swear that they would never enter his rest if not to those who disobeyed?* (HEBREWS 3:17–18)

Apparently this had happened to a lot of people until one courageous young lady took me aside and asked me what sin I thought she had committed!

Having realized how easily I am able unintentionally to offend others, I determine not to take offence when others appear to offend me. I give them the benefit of the doubt. I choose to think well of them. Conflict is a normal part of everyday life – it's how you handle it that makes all the difference.

Discipline and judgment

So if I'm not to be someone else's conscience, what should I do when someone keeps sinning? Should I just ignore it? Are there ever occasions when I should confront another Christian? Jesus said this:

> *Do not judge, or you too will be judged. For in the same way as you judge others, you will be judged, and with the measure you use, it will be measured to you.* (MATTHEW 7:1)

However, Paul talks about disciplining Christians who do wrong. For example:

> *Brothers, if someone is caught in a sin, you who are spiritual should restore him gently.* (GALATIANS 6:1)

How can we reconcile the fact that we are told not to judge with this instruction to carry out discipline? Judgment and discipline are different things. As we saw earlier, judgment is always related to *character*. Discipline, however, is always related to *behaviour*. Discipline has to be based on something we have seen or heard. If we personally observe another Christian sinning against us, the Bible tells us to confront the person alone – the objective of this is to win them back to the Lord. If they don't repent, then we are to take along two or three other witnesses who observed the same sin. If they still won't listen, then we are to tell the church (Matthew 18:15–17). The purpose of this process is not to condemn them, but to restore them to Christ. If there are no other witnesses, it's just your word against theirs. Simply leave it at that. God knows all about it and it's his role to bring conviction, not ours. He will deal with it in his perfect wisdom.

We are so often tempted to judge character, however. Suppose I catch a fellow Christian telling an obvious lie, and I confront them. I could say, 'You're a liar!' but actually that would be judgment because I would have impugned their character. It would be much better to say, 'You have just said something untrue,' which simply calls attention to sinful behaviour that I have personally observed.

If the difference between the two phrases seems too subtle, take some time to think it through: the first phrase implies that he has the identity of a liar, that his character is that of a liar. In short, it implies that deep down inside he is bad and leaves little hope that he could change. The second phrase says nothing about his identity or character. It just calls out a behaviour issue. It leaves plenty of hope for the future.

In fact, perhaps it would be even better to say, 'You're *not* a liar. So why did you just tell a lie?' The truth is that this is a child of God who has just acted out of character. Helping him realize that it's acting out of character gives real hope for positive change.

Calling somebody 'a liar', 'stupid', 'clumsy', 'proud', or 'evil' is an attack on character. It leaves people with no way forward and no resolution because they can't instantly change their character.

If, on the other hand, you point out someone's sinful behaviour to them, you are giving them something that they can work with: 'You're right. What I just said wasn't true, and I'm sorry I said it. Will you forgive me?' That puts an end to the issue there and then, but attacking another person's character can cause lasting damage.

Ephesians 4:29 says: 'Do not let any unwholesome talk come out of your mouths, but only what is helpful for building others up according to their needs, that it may benefit those who listen.' The next verse says, 'And do not grieve the Holy Spirit of God.' It grieves God when we use words that tear one another down instead of using words to build each other up. If you have taken hold of your freedom in Christ you are free to make the right choice in any situation.

Discipline and punishment

There is also a major difference between discipline and punishment. Punishment is related to the Old Testament concept of 'an eye for an eye'. It looks backwards to the past. Discipline, however, looks forwards to the future. Hebrews 12:5–11 tells us that God's discipline is a proof of his love. If we are not being disciplined by God, the Bible says we are illegitimate children of God (verse 8). In the same way, we discipline others because we love them, in order to help them make better choices in the future – not to punish them for the past.

A few years ago I went through a period of intense difficulty just as Freedom In Christ Ministries was being established in the UK. My business that had been supporting us hit a brick wall financially and it seemed that the only way forward would be to close it down and sell our home to meet the debts. Some looked at the circumstances and concluded that God was punishing me for some sin.

God does not punish Christians. The punishment we deserved fell on Christ. He may, however, discipline us so that we don't make the same mistake again and to develop our character:

> *No discipline seems pleasant at the time, but painful. Later on, however, it produces a harvest of righteousness and peace for those who have been trained by it.* (HEBREWS 12:11)

The point of discipline is to help someone become more like Jesus, not to punish them for behaving badly.

Again, if that appears to be a subtle difference, it's worth taking the time to think it through. How wonderful that we don't have a God who punishes us. Instead we have a God who loves us so much that he sometimes makes the hard choice of putting us through difficult circumstances in order to prepare us for the future.

As our character becomes more and more like that of

Jesus, we will increasingly be prepared to offer loving discipline to those who need it rather than simply shrugging our shoulders and leaving them to their own devices.

When we are attacked

What about when the boot is on the other foot: how do we respond if someone attacks our character? Should we be defensive? We will certainly be tempted to be.

At the same time as the business was struggling, someone close to me turned against me and started attacking my character. Accusations were flying everywhere saying essentially that I was proud. Now, I could find some truth in that – actually, as I mentioned earlier, quite a lot of truth – and the Lord was able to use the accusations to develop my character. But the problem was that, rather than pointing out examples of proud behaviour that I could have acknowledged and repented of, this was a pure attack on my character: 'You're proud.' There was no way I could bring it to an end. Worse, I knew that all sorts of things were being said to others that, to me, did not seem true at all. I wanted to go to them and justify myself and denounce my attacker. But it came at the time when I was just getting hold of these concepts myself and I knew that that was not the way forward.

How did Jesus react when it happened to him? 'When they hurled their insults at him, he did not retaliate. When he suffered, he made no threats. Instead, he entrusted himself to him who judges justly' (1 Peter 2:23).

I knew that I had to do the same: entrust myself to God and leave the outcome with him. Now that we are alive in Christ and forgiven, we don't need to defend ourselves any more. If you are wrong, you don't have a defence. If you are right, you don't need one. Christ is our defence. Guess what… Despite many negative things that were said, no one turned against me in any way and the ministry was not damaged. God proved to me at that point that he is well able to defend me and that I really don't have to do it myself.

If you can learn not to be defensive when someone exposes your character defects or attacks your performance, you may have an opportunity to turn the situation around and minister to that person.

I thought that being in Christian ministry would all be sweetness and light. I've since learned that conflict in ministry is normal – it's how you handle it that matters. I once had someone build up all sorts of wrong impressions of things I'd done, and they came and dumped them on me in a big heap, while at the same time admitting that they had also been listed in e-mails sent to various other Christian leaders.

I really wanted to say, 'Who have you sent them to? Write another e-mail right now, taking it all back!' But, of course, it was too late by then. And in any case, this person still believed them. Knowing that I no longer have to defend myself, I simply let them share all of the things and kept quiet until everything was out on the table – it took some time as there was quite a lot of it and I was tempted to defend myself at every point! At the end I thanked them for sharing it, commending them for the courage it must have taken, and assured them of my goodwill towards them. The other person then started to cry and said, 'It's not you, it's me', and I was able to minister to them.

It's important to understand that nobody tears down another person from a position of strength. Those who are critical of others are either hurting or immature. If we are secure in our own identity in Christ, we can learn not to be defensive when they attack us, which may well lead to an opportunity to minister to them.

Authority and accountability

When you picture God the Father, does he resemble a head-master figure looking sternly at you, seeing if there is anything to discipline you for, or is he more like a smiling dad with open arms, waiting for you to run into them, no matter what has happened?

How you answer that question reveals a lot about how you understand ministry, marriage and parenting. Paul wrote, 'While we were still sinners, Christ died for us' (Romans 5:8). Acceptance came first, and then affirmation: 'The Spirit himself testifies with our spirit that we are God's children' (Romans 8:16).

The devil is determined to distort our image of God so that we get this back to front. How on earth can I approach a consuming fire? How can I go to a holy God as a sinner? But if you know God as your loving Father and you know that he accepts you just as you are and loves you no matter what you have done, you can walk boldly into his presence and pour your heart out to him.

Authority figures whose primary characteristic is acceptance will find that they are much more effective than those whose primary characteristic is accountability. If authority figures demand accountability without giving affirmation and acceptance, they will never get it. People under oppressive authority may comply externally under duress, but they will never share anything on an intimate level. People will, however, voluntarily submit to someone in authority who is first of all accepting and affirming.

Suppose a teenager comes home later than promised. Her parent, who has probably been worrying, responds in an overbearing way (in effect saying, 'I make the rules round here!') and asks angrily, 'Where have you been?' The teenager will probably say just one word: 'Out!' To which the parent responds, 'What were you doing?' And the teenager will respond with another word: 'Nothing!' Not a lot of meaningful communication has actually taken place!

In the Gospels you never read about Jesus saying anything like this: 'Now look here! I am the Son of God, so get your act together!' Now, he *is* God, and he *is* the ultimate authority, but he came to us as a gentle shepherd. Yet, after he preached the Sermon on the Mount, 'The crowds were amazed at his teaching, because he taught as one who had authority, and not as their teachers of the law' (Matthew 7:28b–29). This authority did not come from his position but from his character.

When we see people who are struggling with sin we need to learn to be like God. Then we will come alongside them with an attitude of acceptance rather than rejection, without a shred of condemnation but filled with love.

A young lady landed up in our office after more than a decade in and out of mental institutions suffering from anorexia compounded by drug and alcohol addiction. She quickly found her freedom from the anorexia in a local church using our principles, but the addictions were harder to shift. Occasionally she'd slip up. Guess who she called when she was drunk... Always me! Why? Because I would never get cross with her or condemn her but always assured her that Jesus still loved her and that nothing fundamental had changed.

'But doesn't that just encourage her to do it again?' you may ask. That might seem logical, but actually just the opposite is true. If you get cross or condemn her, it just pushes her further away from Jesus and she turns to the drink or drugs again. If you assure her of the truth that there is no condemnation, she can pick herself up off the floor, confess her sins, kick the enemy out of her life and come straight back to her heavenly Father, who gladly accepts her into his presence through his grace.

There was a time when I used to think that few people had major issues. Why? No one talked to me about them – I guess they sensed that I would condemn inwardly if not outwardly. Nowadays people talk to me all the time about the most intimate details of their lives. What changed? Me!

Expressing our needs

If we have needs in a relationship that are not being met, should we suffer in silence or is it OK to express them?

We can express them because we need to walk in the light

and be honest in our relationships. However, we need to be very careful how we express them. The problem is that it can all too easily come out as criticism rather than as a need. A need must be stated as a need, and not a judgment. Suppose a wife doesn't feel loved. She might say to her husband, 'You don't love me any more, do you?' You can almost hear the husband respond, 'Of course I do!' And that's the end of that. It wasn't stated as a need but as judgment of her husband's character.

Suppose she said, 'I just don't feel loved right now, and I need to be.' By turning the 'you' judgment to an 'I' need, she has expressed her need without blaming anybody. Her husband now has the opportunity to meet that need and is highly disposed to do so.

To illustrate further, consider a husband who doesn't feel needed. Instead of saying, 'You make me feel useless,' he could express his need by saying, 'I feel so unimportant.' By changing from a 'you' accusation to an 'I' need, the message is received without blame, and the other person is more predisposed to help.

We reap what we sow

Jesus said, 'It is more blessed to give than to receive' (Acts 20:35), which at first glance seems nonsensical. How can it feel better to give to someone else than to get something oneself? Have you tried it?

The bizarre thing is that when you do something for someone else, it feels great! When you help somebody else, you help yourself in the process. Jesus said in Luke 6:38:

Give and it will be given to you. A good measure, pressed down, shaken together and running over, will be poured into your lap. For with the measure you use, it will be measured to you.

If you want somebody to love you, love somebody. If you want a friend, be a friend. We really do get out of life what we put into it. It's a biblical principle. I remember as a child being asked to do various chores by my parents. Often I simply did the bare minimum – just enough to get them off my back. It didn't feel that great. However, on the rare occasion when I determined to help properly and went beyond what I could get away with, not only were my parents delighted but I felt really good. If we do just enough to 'get by', the truth is, we are robbing ourselves.

We all have needs. We all need to be loved, accepted and affirmed. Let's not wait for people to love, accept and affirm us. Let's go and see whom we can love, accept and affirm. Call someone. Or are you waiting for somebody to call you? It may never happen.

Much of our character development comes from our relationships with others. Whether we get on with them or always seem to clash with them, they help us become more like Jesus if we learn to handle the relationships well. Yes, even that really difficult person who gets right up your nose is helping you accomplish God's overriding objective for your life: to make you more and more like Jesus in character. Next time you meet them, maybe you'll want to give them a great big hug to say thanks!

God's Goal for His Bride

So, in helping others we help ourselves. In meeting others' needs, we feel better ourselves. However, there is a great paradox. If we help others *in order to* help ourselves or meet others' needs *in order to* feel better, it doesn't work. Helping ourselves is a by-product of sincerely wanting to help someone else, of choosing to love them, of becoming more like Jesus.

It is all too easy to get caught up with the world's preoccupation with self. We can read books like this to enable us to feel better, be a 'successful Christian' or whatever. But that would be to aim far lower than Jesus would have us aim. As our character becomes more and more like his, we will have a deeper joy and a greater enjoyment of life. But if we are aiming at those things in themselves, it won't happen.

We do not live the Christian life in isolation. We are part of the church. What is God's goal for his Bride?

> *His intent was that now, through the church, the manifold wisdom of God should be made known to the rulers and authorities in the heavenly realms.* (EPHESIANS 3:10)

The purpose of the church of which you and I are an integral part is to demonstrate God's wisdom. To whom? To the rulers and authorities – Paul is not talking about the president or the prime minister here but about demonic powers. Where? In the heavenly realms, that is to say in the spiritual world that we cannot see but which is just as real as the physical world that we can see.

Those of us brought up in the West with its 'modern'

worldview have been programmed to overlook the reality of the spiritual world. Even though we acknowledge it theologically, the way we live our lives and conduct our ministries may tell a different story. Yet the spiritual battle forms a backcloth to the entire Bible, from the garden in Genesis right through to the final battle in the Book of Revelation.

When Paul wrote the verses quoted above, he was talking about his own calling from God which he described a couple of verses previously as 'to preach to the Gentiles the unsearchable riches of Christ'. He was playing his part in what is often called 'the Great Commission', the command that Jesus gave to the whole church in Matthew 28:19–20:

> *Therefore go and make disciples of all nations, baptising them in the name of the Father and of the Son and of the Holy Spirit, and teaching them to obey everything I have commanded you.*

So, against the backdrop of a battle between God and Satan, God's purpose is that his amazing wisdom will be made known to Satan's evil demonic forces *through the church* as we go into all the world and make disciples.

All power and authority

Every time we display Christ's character, it's a demonstration of God's wisdom in the heavenly realms. Satan hates it. Every time someone becomes a Christian, it's a demonstration of God's wisdom in the heavenly realms. Satan hates it.

What, however, is stopping many people out there from becoming Christians? If we don't see the whole of reality and overlook the reality of the spiritual world, we might answer that by saying something like, 'No one is going out there and telling them' or 'We are not engaging properly with them and showing them Jesus in a way they can understand' or 'The church puts them off'. There is truth and value in those statements. However, we might miss a major issue:

> *The god of this age has blinded the minds of unbelievers, so that they cannot see the light of the gospel of the glory of Christ, who is the image of God.*   (2 CORINTHIANS 4:4)

The main reason why people do not see the truth and turn to Christ is because the enemy has 'blinded their minds'. That's why you can sit down with someone and explain the truth and be met with a blank, uncomprehending stare. If we are to make more disciples, we need first to overcome this issue.

Do we have to put up with Satan blinding minds? Paul tells us that we have been blessed in the heavenly realms with *every* spiritual blessing in Christ (Ephesians 1:3). And look at the context of Jesus' Great Commission:

> *Then Jesus came to them and said, 'All authority in heaven and on earth has been given to me. Therefore go and make disciples of all nations.'*

The reason he could send us out to make disciples is that he had been given all authority in heaven and on earth, another clear allusion to the unseen spiritual world. In this statement he confers that authority on us. How can anything stop us? Satan in and of himself certainly cannot. Jesus said:

> *When a strong man, fully armed, guards his own house, his possessions are safe. But when someone stronger attacks and overpowers him, he takes away the armour in which the man trusted and divides up the spoils.*   (LUKE 11:21–22)

In this analogy Satan is the strong man. You wouldn't dream of attacking him or plundering his possessions unless he was out of action.

And having disarmed the powers and authorities, he made a
public spectacle of them, triumphing over them by the cross.

(COLOSSIANS 2:15)

Christ has disarmed Satan. He is roundly defeated. In fact, Christ has triumphed over him by the cross. He has tied the strong man up. That is why Jesus can say, 'I will build my church, and the gates of Hades will not prevail against it' (Matthew 16:18).

Are you getting the picture of just how much power and authority we have to fulfil the goal that God has for the church? You would think that Satan would struggle to maintain that spiritual blindness in the face of overwhelming power and authority from the church.

The early church

In fact, that's just how it looked in the early days of the church. They operated in a world that was far more openly hostile than the one we operate in. But they went out and preached the gospel and thousands of people became Christians in just a small area – 3,000 people in one place on just one day. Within 400 years the mighty Roman Empire had fallen to Christianity.

Satan would have you believe that the church stopped growing long ago and is now in terminal decline. Is that how it feels to you? Nothing could be further from the truth. We are part of the most dynamic movement the world has ever seen. The church of Jesus Christ has been growing massively ever since he founded it and in recent years its growth has accelerated hugely. It is estimated that by 1900 the number of dedicated believers had grown from 0 per cent when Jesus started it to 2.5 per cent of the world's population. The next 70 years (1900 to 1970) saw that percentage double to 5 per cent. Then between 1970 and 2000, it rose to a staggering 11.2 per cent, even against the background of an exploding world population, which in the twentieth century rose from 1.65 billion to 6 billion.[1]

According to the United Nations, it took until 1804 for the world's population to reach 1 billion. At that time there would have been around 20 million Christians in the world. Nowadays that many are added to the church every four to five months. It is estimated that more Christians are alive right now than all who have died in the previous 2,000 years.

Where is all this taking place? In Africa only 3 per cent of the population were Christians in 1900. Now it's around 45 per cent. South Korea has been officially reclassified by the United Nations from a Buddhist nation to a Christian one. In China, where believers are still sometimes imprisoned and even die for their beliefs, it is estimated that the church numbers around 100 million people.

So why has the church in the West been in decline? This is clearly an abnormal situation, an historical anomaly. Why is it that the early church saw such results and we do not? What has changed?

Has the enemy got more evil or powerful? No. As I travel around, I meet a lot of people who tell me that they live in a particularly 'difficult' or 'dark' area. Well, they are right, because the whole world lies in the power of the evil one (1 John 5:19). But surely your area cannot be worse than the one the early church operated in as they went out beyond Judea. Go to the ruins of Corinth, Ephesus or other cities from that time and you will find evidence of a heavily occult environment where there were offerings being made to idols (demons), temple prostitutes and other nasty sin. Sin in the communities we operate in clearly should not stop us.

Have people out there changed? Fundamentally human beings are the same. Without Christ they were and are 'objects of wrath' (Ephesians 2:3).

Has God changed? Is it that he has decided not to pour

out so much of his Spirit? Has he decided not to act? Is he not doing what he did in those early days? No! 'Jesus Christ is the same yesterday and today and forever' (Hebrews 13:8), and he 'wants all men to be saved and to come to a knowledge of the truth' (1 Timothy 2:4).

The problem is that in the West we have inherited a compromised church. The exciting thing is that we can do something about it. In fact, if we all took seriously the goal that God has for our lives, to become more and more like Jesus in character, and lived out the consequences of that in our relationships with one another, we would see a dramatic difference.

We are all part of one body

In John 17 Jesus prayed for those who would come to believe in him through his disciples' message – that's you and me! He could have prayed any number of things for us but he focused on just one. You can be sure that he did not choose this one thing on a whim but made sure that he prayed for the key thing we would need as we work towards fulfilling what God has for us to do. This is what he chose to pray:

> My prayer is not for them alone. I pray also for those who will believe in me through their message, that all of them may be one, Father, just as you are in me and I am in you. May they also be in us so that the world may believe that you have sent me. I have given them the glory that you gave me, that they may be one as we are one: I in them and you in me. May they be brought to complete unity to let the world know that you sent me and have loved them even as you have loved me.
>
> (JOHN 17:20–23)

He chose to pray that we would be one, that we would be brought to complete unity. Why? Why is it that people out there do not believe? Because the enemy has blinded their minds. Here we start to see that the reason why Jesus wants us to be one is 'so that the world may believe'. Can our unity have an effect in the spiritual world? This well-known passage from the Old Testament implies that it can:

> *How good and pleasant it is when brothers live together in unity! It is like precious oil poured on the head, running down on the beard, running down on Aaron's beard, down upon the collar of his robes. It is as if the dew of Hermon were falling on Mount Zion. For there the Lord bestows his blessing, even life for evermore.*   (PSALM 133:1–3)

Where there is unity, the Lord bestows his blessing. A blessing operates at the level of the spiritual world. Jesus gave his followers a new commandment:

> *A new command I give you: Love one another. As I have loved you, so you must love one another. By this all men will know that you are my disciples, if you love one another.*
>
>   (JOHN 13:34–35)

If we love each other, we will be united. If we love each other, 'all men will know that you are my disciples'. There seems to be a relationship between our level of love and unity and the ability Satan has to keep people in spiritual blindness.

Jesus asked the Father that we would be one 'just as you are in me and I am in you'. He was praying that we would become like him. And when he commanded us to love, remember that he *is* love. All he is asking is that we become more and more like him. As this goal is met in our personal lives and we love our fellow-Christians and walk in unity with them, his overall goal for the church is also met: people will be released from spiritual blindness and the wisdom of God will be demonstrated in the heavenly realms.

Knowing this, if you were Satan, what would be your number-one tactic to prevent God's goal for the church being accomplished? What would be the most effective way to keep people in spiritual blindness?

> Therefore each of you must put off falsehood and speak truthfully to his neighbour, for we are all members of one body. 'In your anger do not sin': Do not let the sun go down while you are still angry, and do not give the devil a foothold.
>
> (EPHESIANS 4:25–27)

You would attack the unity of God's people. You would try to tempt them into falling out with each other, into lying to each other, into getting angry with each other, into unforgiveness.

If you have read the first three books in the series, you will have seen this passage from Ephesians quoted on a number of occasions to show how sin can give the enemy a point of influence (a 'foothold') in our individual lives. That is certainly true. However, note the whole context of the passage: it's about being 'members of one body' and the sins mentioned are the type that we are likely to commit against other members of the body. When we do that, we give Satan footholds in the corporate structure of the church itself as well as in our own lives. Even though we have everything we need to fulfil God's goal, we can choose to allow Satan to hold us back.

That is why so much demonic activity is concentrated on trying to make us fall out with each other, emphasize our differences, put truth above grace. When we realize that we are not fighting flesh and blood, that so much hangs on this, then surely it will become of first importance to us.

Some twenty-five years ago, I felt a compulsion to pray into the night and keep asking the Lord to share his heart with me. After quite a while I saw two pictures very clearly one after the other – I haven't experienced anything quite like it since.

There was a huge field of wheat ready to harvest. In one

corner was a man cutting the wheat with a scythe. He worked and worked but hardly made any impression. It was obvious that he was only going to harvest a tiny part of the potential of that field. Then I saw that in the farmyard was a brand-new combine harvester, the sort that could have done the whole job in a couple of hours. But it couldn't be used because it was in pieces – all its parts were scattered over the farmyard.

Then I saw a picture of a huge gushing waterfall coming over a cliff. A huge amount of water. Yet the riverbed at the bottom was dry and because no water was flowing out, the land was a desert where nothing was growing. The reason there was no water was because there were deep fissures in the river-bed and the water was simply disappearing into them. I said, 'What do you want me to do, Lord?' and I saw some of the fissures join together, and as they did so, some of the water ran down the river-bed and irrigated the land. Then plants began to grow.

The meaning of these pictures was very clear to me at the time. If God's people are not working together, we will only ever reach a tiny part of the harvest. And even though God is pouring out his Spirit upon us, it will have no great effect if we are divided. We can pray to the Lord to save people and pray for him to send his Spirit upon us, but he says to us, 'You already have everything you need. I am already pouring out my Spirit. But if you are not working together, there is nothing more I can do.' We don't need to ask God for 'more'. We already have everything we need and we simply need to play our part.

The staggering conclusion we can reach when it comes to seeing people come to Christ is that it is not so much the sin 'out there' that is stopping them seeing the truth but the sin 'in here' in the church.

The early church, of course, was not hampered by corporate sin or disunity, at least for a while. That is why they could simply go out, preach the word and see so many respond. The answer has always been the same. This is what God said to his people in the Old Testament:

> *When I shut up the heavens so that there is no rain, or command locusts to devour the land or send a plague among my people, if my people, who are called by my name, will humble themselves and pray and seek my face and turn from their wicked ways, then will I hear from heaven and will forgive their sin and will heal their land.* (2 CHRONICLES 7:13–14)

When there was a problem caused by their sin, the answer for God's people was to humble themselves, pray, seek God's face and deal with their sin.

Although the state of the Western church is not good, I remain encouraged. I travel reasonably widely and meet a lot of leaders. Increasingly I am meeting people who genuinely value unity and are working hard for it. City-wide movements are springing up in which leaders are coming together in an unforced way simply because they want to demonstrate unity. It is not unity based on compromise but on the recognition that we are the body of Christ and each part has a crucial role to play. I believe that we will increasingly see groups of leaders from all across the church leading their people in prayer and repentance to get rid of the footholds of the enemy. Then we will see that the gates of Hades really do have no chance against the Bride of Christ.

See you at the feast

Do you see just how important it is that you and I adopt the goal of becoming more and more like Jesus? He delights in you as you are transformed little by little, day by day into the likeness of Jesus. He has done everything he needs to do to make that possible, including sending his Son to die for you and delegating all power and authority in heaven and earth to us so that we can make disciples. Nothing and no one can stop you becoming all that he wants you to be. But it's not simply an individual thing.

As we all choose that path, we will not be able to help but work for true unity. We will genuinely love each other. We will want the best for each other. We will consider each other's needs above our own. We will be secure enough in Christ not to compete. We will handle conflict well.

Our unity will have a dramatic effect on those who do not believe. Many, many more will find that their spiritual blindness disappears and they will know the truth that will set them free.

As this happens, we will be fulfilling God's goal, to demonstrate his wisdom through the church in the heavenly realms. We will be preparing ourselves for his return. Revelation 19:7–8 says this:

> Let us rejoice and be glad and give him glory! For the wedding of the Lamb has come, and his bride has made herself ready. Fine linen, bright and clean, was given her to wear. (Fine linen stands for the righteous acts of the saints.)

We are each part of the Bride of Christ or, more accurately at this point, his Bride-to-be. The wedding feast of the Lamb is the most exciting event that will ever happen and we are going to be there! No matter what she looks like right now, the church is going to be beautiful and all eyes will be on her. She will have prepared herself.

Jewish marriage customs involved a number of traditions. When the young man had found the woman of his dreams, he presented his offer of marriage to her and to her father along with a dowry. He would then pour a cup of wine, which was symbolic of a blood covenant, and waited anxiously to see if she drank it. If she did, she signified her acceptance of the proposal and they were betrothed.

The young man would then give her gifts and leave. Before leaving he would announce, 'I am going to prepare a place for you', a phrase Jesus spoke to his disciples (John 14:2), and 'I will return for you when it is ready' (see John 14:3).

The bride would set about making herself ready so that she would be pure and beautiful for her bridegroom while he returned to his father's house to prepare the wedding chamber. He had to do a very thorough job and get his father's approval before it could be considered ready. If anyone asked the date of the wedding, all he could say was, 'Only my father knows' (see Matthew 24:36 for Jesus' equivalent statement).

When the father agreed that the chamber was ready, the bridegroom could collect his bride. The tradition was that this was done at night. It usually happened around a year after the betrothal but the bride was not told in advance exactly when it would take place. It was the custom that she would keep a lamp, her veil and her other things beside her bed so that she would be ready when he finally came for her. Her bridesmaids were also waiting and had to have oil ready for their lamps (see Matthew 25:1–13 for Jesus' parable based on this). Imagine the excitement and sense of anticipation!

When the groom and his friends got close to the bride's house they would give a shout and blow a ram's horn to let her know they were approaching. She would hurriedly put on the clothes that she had prepared and go with them to the father's house.

When they arrived, the first thing that happened was that the bridegroom and the bride would go into the wedding chamber and consummate the marriage. The groom's best friend stood outside waiting for the groom to tell him that the marriage had been consummated. The proof of this was the bed-sheet bearing the blood shed by the bride as a result of her first sexual intercourse. This was a sign of purity before marriage and also again of a blood covenant.

This was the signal for celebrations. When the couple emerged there would be much congratulation and the marriage supper could begin. The celebrations typically lasted a whole week.

The church is now at the point of betrothal, waiting for the Bridegroom to come and get her and take her back to his

Father's house, to the place where the marriage will be consummated. Then there will be celebrations for a thousand years!

Right at the start of the first book in this series I wrote this:

> Although it may sound as if this book is about you, in fact it's really about *Jesus Christ* – what he has done, who he is, his astonishing resources, his Kingdom purposes and the exciting place he has called you to occupy in them. It's about knowing him for the wonderful person he is so that we can simply fall at his feet and offer him ourselves completely and utterly.
>
> A time is coming when there is going to be a feast the like of which has never been experienced before. The trumpets will sound and the Bridegroom, Jesus, will come for his Bride, the church. She will have made herself ready for him and will be dressed in fine linen. There will be a wedding feast and a new age will be ushered in. You are going to be there.

As you adopt God's goal for your life to become more and more like Jesus in character and as you learn how to work with fellow-Christians in love and unity, you are playing your part in making the Bride ready.

Without Christ we are people of no account, no great wisdom, no power, no real hope of impacting our communities, no hope of growing in character. But with Christ in us, we have the most significant role imaginable in future history. All eyes are on us. With Christ in us we are immensely significant and powerful.

So, what about the 'next nine holes' of your life?

Will you adopt the personal goal of becoming more and more like Jesus in character and ensure that every other goal in your life is consistent with that?

Will you choose to spend the rest of your life building with 'gold, silver and precious stones'?

Will you rejoice in the difficulties you face because they help you towards your goal?

Are you ready to work wholeheartedly with those God has put alongside you in his body, the church, even if they rub you up the wrong way?

Will you make true unity an absolute priority, refusing point blank to cooperate with Satan's temptations to criticize, gossip and rebel?

If so, you can be everything God created you to be – and you will play your part in preparing the Bride for 'the Day'.

No matter what your past or present circumstances, nothing and no one can stop you becoming the person God planned – except you.

Everything is still to play for!

NOTE

1. Source: church statistics assembled by the Lausanne Statistical Task Force.

FREEDOM IN CHRIST

Discipleship Series

Free to Be Yourself
ISBN: 978-1-85424-857-2

Win the Daily Battle
ISBN: 978-1-85424-858-9

Break Free, Stay Free
ISBN: 978-1-85424-859-6

The You God Planned
ISBN: 978-1-85424-860-2

These four short volumes can be read individually but also form a valuable accompaniment to the Freedom In Christ course.

Many Christians end up acting as they think a Christian should act – and finding that they simply can't keep it up. They either drop out or burn out. True fruitfulness comes from realizing that we became someone completely new the moment we became Christians. Living out the truth of who we now are makes all the difference.

The 'eternal life' that Jesus came to give us is not just something we get when we die. It's a whole different quality of life right now, a life which gives us perfect acceptance, phenomenal significance and complete security. Know the truth and choose to believe it and you can be the person you were made to be.

Available from your local Christian bookshop.

In case of difficulty, please visit the Lion Hudson website: *www. lionhudson.com*

Freedom In Christ In The UK

Church leaders – can we help you make disciples?

Although the Church may have made some *converts*, most will agree that we have made few real *disciples*. Far too many Christians struggle to take hold of basic biblical truth and *live it out*. It's not as if we lack excellent teaching programmes. It's more to do with people's ability to "connect" with truth. Or, as Jesus put it, "You will *know* the truth and the truth will set you free." (John 8:32)

Many churches in the UK now use the Freedom In Christ approach to help Christians make connections with truth and mature into fruitful disciples. It works well as: a church-wide discipleship programme using The Freedom In Christ Discipleship Course; a follow-up to introductory courses like Alpha; a cell equipping track; or a small group study.

If you are a UK church leader, we are at your disposal. We run a regular programme of conferences and training, and are always happy to offer advice.

Send for our catalogue

Send for our full colour catalogue of books, videos and audiocassettes. It includes resources for churches and for individuals (including children and young people and specialist areas such as depression and addiction).

Join the Freedom Fellowship

For those using the Freedom In Christ approach, the Freedom Fellowship provides advice on getting started in your church and regular news and encouragement.

For details of any of the above, see www.ficm.org.uk, e-mail info@ficm.org.uk or write to us at:
Freedom In Christ Ministries, PO Box 2842, READING RG2 9RT.

www.**ficm**.org.uk

Freedom In Christ Ministries is a company limited by guarantee (number 3984116) and a registered charity (number 1082555). It works by equipping local churches to help Christians claim their freedom in Christ and become fruitful disciples.

Made in the USA
Coppell, TX
13 September 2022

83054110R00067